LOVE
IS PATIENT
LOVE
IS KIND

LOVE
IS PATIENT
LOVE
IS KIND

Inspiration and Meditations *for* Brides

CANDY CHAND

FAIR WINDS
PRESS
GLOUCESTER, MASSACHUSETTS

NOTE:

All Scripture references are taken from the King James Version of the Bible except where otherwise noted. In order to protect the privacy of some of the individuals mentioned throughout this book, their names have been changed.

Text © 2003 by Candy Chand

First published in the USA in 2003 by
Fair Winds Press
33 Commercial Street
Gloucester, MA 01930

Library of Congress Cataloging-in-Publication Data available

ISBN 1-59233-020-7

10 9 8 7 6 5 4 3 2 1

Cover design by Yee Design
Book design by Yee Design

Printed and bound in China

To Patrick, with love

CONTENTS

Dear Laura,

May our Lord always guide you and Alex clearly throughout this life!

Love,
Aunt Liz

If I speak with tongues of men and of angels, but have not love, I am only a resounding gong or a clanging cymbal. If I have the gift of prophecy and can fathom all mysteries and all knowledge, and if I have a faith that can move mountains, but have not love, I am nothing. If I give all I possess to the poor and surrender my body to the flames, but have not love, I gain nothing.

Love is patient, love is kind. It does not envy, it does not boast, it is not proud. It is not rude, it is not self-seeking, it is not easily angered, it keeps no record of wrongs. Love does not delight in evil but rejoices with the truth. It always protects, always trusts, always hopes, always perseveres.

Love never fails...

1 CORINTHIANS 13:1–8
(New International Version)

INTRODUCTION

The Scriptures are filled with joyous expressions of love.
Although often contrary to what we find within the pages
of dime-store romance novels, true love, as it's revealed in
the Bible, is genuine and eternal. Is it any wonder, then,
that 1 Corinthians 13 contains such beloved, and often
quoted, verses? For it's there that we find the sacred virtues
elevated far above the rest.

Yes, among all the world's riches, the greatest of these is love.

I.

LOVE IS PATIENT

Patience—hardly an easy virtue to master. With a hurried world pushing firmly behind us, tight deadlines looming before us, and overburdened schedules threatening to cause even the calmest individuals to snap, is it any wonder that when it comes to love, we're also in a rush? Yet love takes time. It takes time to find love and to be certain we've discovered the one individual we wish to spend our lives with in a forever relationship. It takes time for love to grow, and it takes time to build a relationship that will stand the rough and rocky road upon which life will surely send us traveling.

DON'T HURRY LOVE

Sharon met her husband, James, when she was in her late 20s. Well-meaning people (mostly Sharon's sweet grandmother) had been pushing her for years to hook up with someone, anyone, so she could move on with her life before it was "too late." It wasn't fear that had made Sharon wait. It was her pure determination not to settle. Sharon wanted to be sure. And the men she'd seen before her husband hadn't impressed her in the least. No, she was not waiting for a millionaire (her husband smiles at the thought) or for anyone perfect; Sharon simply wanted someone who was right for her.

At one holiday gathering, Sharon's grandmother pointed to a friend of the family who'd hooked up at the ripe old age of 19. Yes, she was married all right, and she stood tall in the center of the room, proudly displaying her wedding band, with a darling little baby in her arms and a doting husband hovering nearby. Sound picture-perfect? Not really. Hold on, because here's where it gets really interesting: Her loving husband also happened to be an ex-convict and an active drug addict. Got the full image now? Sharon's grandmother, oblivious to the dire situation this young teen had gotten herself into, simply used this gathering as a strange opportunity to point out that if this young girl could manage to find someone at 19, why couldn't Sharon, being years older, do the same?

For Sharon, despite having to go to many friends' weddings over the years (sometimes for the second go-around), feeling she stood out as the last single person on earth, and garnering looks from her ever doubtful but well-meaning grandmother, she continued to stand her ground. What was her plan, you ask? She would be patient. The right person would eventually come along.

In the meantime, she discovered something valuable about herself. Through patience, through giving God time, she was also becoming a better person. Sharon learned over the years to discover who she really was, what she really wanted out of life, and what her beliefs truly were. She began to grasp the details of her standards and priorities. In fact, by the time Sharon did meet her husband, he wasn't just right for her; she was also right for him.

Rest assured, patience doesn't always require years of waiting. For some, goals and dreams may progress rather quickly. Finding the right person to marry doesn't have to take forever. Some folks discover love at a much younger age, but on some level, to maintain that blessed relationship, they will still be required to accept and desire the virtue of patience. Ask those who've been married for many years, and they will tell you that they wrestled with patience until they finally understood that this virtue must be embraced, not fought.

Once you meet the one you're sure is right for you and decide to make a lifelong commitment, you may choose a long engagement or a quick one— whichever is suitable for you. There's no wrong or right choice. In my case, I met my husband, Patrick, in August. We were engaged by New Year's and married the following July. I know it was rather fast by some standards, but I was already in my late 20s, and by that time, I had certainly kissed my share of toads. I felt like an expert when it came to my personal expectations, and I knew a good man when I saw one.

I've met wonderful couples who were married soon after meeting, and many are happily united to this very day. It's proof that there are no absolutes regarding the timing of love. Others chose long engagements that worked beautifully for them as well. So, whatever you've decided, just make sure that in your world, in your book, and by your own standards, you're not being rushed. Be certain that you are exhibiting the virtue of patience and that you understand that all good things will be fulfilled in due time. Finally, rather than going your way and simply asking God to bless your already finalized decisions, give him the opportunity to speak up, to shout a resounding no, and to tell you to turn in another direction if necessary. This, in particular, is where patience comes into play. We ask. We wait. And most importantly, we obey that still, small voice inside each of us—the very voice of God.

❦

Marriages are made in heaven. But, again,
so are thunder, lightning, tornadoes, and hail.

UNKNOWN

❦

No one is perfect. We should never expect from others what we're obviously unable to deliver ourselves. Fine-tuning the details of a relationship takes time, and some issues never truly get resolved.

When my husband and I were dating, I began to wonder about his grasp of basic Scripture. This was important to me, and I wondered if he shared my same level of interest. So, I did what I am famous for and began to drill him with a slew of Bible questions. Looking back, I feel silly, but at the time, my makeshift spiritual test made perfect sense to me. (My husband, by the way, has learned over the years that there's no winning these kinds of games.) When, unfortunately, his answers fell short of what I'd hoped for, he saw my obvious disappointment, looked at me, and said, "You know, Candy. If you plant an apple tree in the backyard today, you can't expect it to bear fruit by tomorrow morning. These things take time." Knowing that at that moment my husband was not familiar with any Bible verses, I realized there was a deeper message for me from above:

And why beholdest thou the mote that is in thy brother's eye, but perceivest not the beam that is in thine own eye? Either how canst thou say to thy brother, Brother, let me pull out the mote that is in thine eye, when thou thyself beholdest not the beam that is in thine own eye? Thou

hypocrite, cast out first the beam out of thine own eye, and then shalt thou see clearly to pull out the mote that is in thy brother's eye. For a good tree bringeth not forth corrupt fruit; neither doth a corrupt tree bring forth good fruit. For every tree is known by his own fruit. For of thorns, men do not gather figs, nor of a bramble bush gather they grapes. A good man out of the good treasure of his heart bringeth forth that which is good; and an evil man out of the evil treasure of his heart bringeth forth that which is evil; for of the abundance of the heart his mouth speaketh.

LUKE 6:41-45

જૐ

Yes, growing emotional and even spiritual fruit takes time. Again, we need patience so we don't expect immediate perfection and can therefore take the time to make all things good in our lives.

Many couples learn over the years which hot buttons never to push. We're all sensitive about certain areas of our existence, and caring spouses will walk on eggshells when need be. We learn which issues to bring forth, even if it's repeatedly, to resolve them over time; which issues to avoid; and which ones to ignore. The old expression "Don't sweat the small stuff" frequently applies to marriage.

Have patience for change in your spouse's life and your own, and work toward those goals, but accept that some things just aren't worth disputing. You decide what the priorities are and enjoy your future avoiding squabbles over trivia.

BE PATIENT WITH YOURSELF

As we begin to grant grace to others, allowing them time to grow, offer yourself the same virtue. You are a growing, changing person with lessons to learn and decisions to make—some good and some not so good, but hopefully ones you will gain knowledge from in time. Be patient with yourself as you become a better individual and consequently a better partner.

Are you struggling with your own personal demons and imperfections, whether spiritual, emotional, or physical? Are you attempting yet another diet to force your body into submission? Are you taking another self-help class to better understand who you are? Are you revamping your financial plan because your credit cards can't take one more purchase before the accounts bust? Are you scheduling time with your Creator to better understand your place in his plan? They're all good and noble ideas, but be patient with yourself, understand that change takes time, and don't criticize to the point where failure is certain. Be positive, ask for help, pray for guidance and strength, learn, study, and pursue a better life, but allow yourself the gift of forgiveness for your failures. After all, you'd do the same for others, wouldn't you?

BE PATIENT FOR YOUR DREAMS

We all have goals, dreams, and hopes—as individuals, as couples, and often as families. Having the virtue of patience is vital, not just to help us survive, but also to allow us to joyfully experience the days, months, or years it takes to see those hopes fulfilled.

Perhaps the dream is for a first home, a career, financial stability, or a new baby. Sometimes we receive our blessings immediately, and other times they arrive by sheer determination, sweat, prayer, and faith, after long years of waiting.

Stay in tune with each other, pursue your dreams together. You may share the same goals, or you may just have your own, but either way, support each other. Hope with your spouse, dream with your spouse, and believe you will see your aspirations come to fulfillment. Never let delays or years of waiting bring you to frustration, causing you to become bitter, angry, and resentful or, worse yet, to turn on each other.

Patrick has supported my creative career for more than six years. When I first approached him with the idea of writing a book, he jumped right on my bandwagon. Yes, he has seen my ups and downs. He's viewed my rejection letters as well as my acceptance contracts. He has seen expected royalty statements disappear in a poof, taking a few of my dreams right along with them. However, although I'm sure he's been tempted to ask me to move on, get a real full-time job, and be more realistic, he continues to support my writing because he knows how much joy it brings me. Times have been tough, but Patrick's been patient as we wait together for my writing career to take off. In the meantime, I'm doing what I love, and he sees the difference in me because of it. Patience, for us, has paid off, perhaps not with a big, fat bank account, but in a happier, more fulfilled marriage.

Patience is a necessary ingredient of genius.

BENJAMIN DISRAELI, EARL OF BEACONSFIELD

When my husband and I first married, we wanted children right away. Within six months, and actually the first month I tried, I became pregnant with my daughter, Tiffany. How easy was that? Perfect pregnancy (okay, minus a few serious months of vomiting), perfect delivery (minus some even more serious screaming), and voilà—an absolutely perfect baby girl.

A couple of years later, my husband and I decided it was time for another child. Convinced this would be a piece of cake too, we tried and we conceived, but sadly enough, we miscarried a few months later. Deeply crushed, we eventually pulled ourselves together and counted our blessings— a happy marriage, a beautiful daughter, and a future that would likely include many more healthy children.

No one had prepared me for the possibility that it would take three and a half more years before I'd conceive again. This time, much more aware that life doesn't always go as planned, I walked through my pregnancy with emotional caution.

Fortunately, nine months later, our beautiful, healthy son, Nicholas, was born. Yes, we required far more patience to conceive our second baby than we needed for our first, but the result was the same—two beautiful, healthy children we love more than I can even begin to describe. Life brought us patience through difficulty, but in time, we reaped the rewards of its gracious fruit.

Once our kids were a little older, new concerns came into play. Now we desired to bring our young children to a better neighborhood—one with larger yards, more open space, wildlife, and natural, beautiful surroundings. We waited, we tried, we prayed. Every year, just like clockwork, we'd check the real-estate comps for our neighborhood to see if we were in financial shape to make the move. Year after year, we'd look at nearby communities, size them up, compare their value, and come to the same conclusion: The timing was just not right. I can't tell you how often we waited, we prayed, and we hoped that our dream would finally happen. But time after time, the answer was a resounding no.

Patience is the best remedy for every trouble.

PLAUTUS

∂℥

Finally, one autumn day after eleven years of trying, the moment was right. We found a perfect home in the perfect community with equally perfect neighbors. It was almost too good to be true. Our home sold immediately, and despite some ugly escrow nightmares, we were on our way. Looking back, I'm grateful we didn't move earlier. After all, our new home wasn't even available then. If we'd moved before, we would have felt compelled to move again. While we waited, God taught us patience, appreciation for what we had, and a deep understanding that in some ways we're powerless to change our future until the timing is truly right.

No matter what you face and no matter what your dreams, goals, or challenges are, you'll find that through patience, instead of constant struggle and strife, grace will bless your marriage.

BE PATIENT FOR FINANCES

Financial disasters are the horrible downfall of many marriages. Although "keeping up with the Joneses" is a common culprit, so is being impatient to accumulate wealth over time. We want instant success, instant gratification, instant wealth, and instant material prizes to flash before the world. Whether we want to be dressed in the best attire, furnish our new apartment with designer merchandise, or buy our dream home, many of us feel compelled to have things before we can really afford them.

Obviously, when our income doesn't meet or exceeds our spending, we all know where that takes us—ca-ching—straight to the credit cards. To avoid the pitfall of outrageous, out-of-control credit card bills, we must first understand why we're driven to attain things instantly and why we have difficulty waiting for our desires. Then we can discipline ourselves through discussion with our spouse, prayer, and inner dialogue to wait with patience for all good and pleasant things instead of purchasing all our dreams via the manipulative gods of plastic.

We must be patient not only with each other and ourselves but also with God, who is there to help in times of need. Is there no one you can talk to? Is there no one on earth who understands your financial and other struggles? Rest assured, the Almighty does and asks that you patiently await his answer.

I waited patiently for the LORD;
And he inclined unto me, and heard my cry
He brought me up also out of an horrible pit, out of the miry clay,
And set my feet upon a rock, and established my goings.
And he hath put a new song in my mouth, even praise unto our God:
Many shall see it, and fear, and shall trust in the LORD.

PSALM 40:1-3

Of course, there's a rational purpose for credit, and I'd never say otherwise, but never allow excessive debt, and the marital stress that often accompanies it, to be the result of your inability to grasp the virtue of patience when it comes to attaining your desires.

BE PATIENT WITH DIFFERENCES

Some differences are deal breakers. Are you involved with an emotionally or physically abusive personality? If so, look inside yourself and ask why you're willing to tolerate such behavior. Then ask for help—from God, from your spiritual advisor, from your friends. It doesn't matter who you turn to, just get assistance. I promise, no matter who you are, you deserve better.

Fortunately, most of us will have to deal with only minor differences in our relationships, such as having dissimilar viewpoints or opposite ways of responding to situations. In these cases, the differences may make our relationships more interesting. After all, who really wants to be married to a clone of herself? Opposites attract. We all know that. Yet sometimes those varying ways of seeing life still cause conflict. When they do, decide which behaviors require action, which require compromise, and which require you to accept that you and your partner are unique and simply see life a little differently.

How many couples do you know who after twenty years of marriage are still fighting over the toothpaste tube? Of course it'd be easy for your partner to roll the tube if it would make you happy. But it would be just as easy for you to get your own toothpaste and move on with your life. Think about it: Is your spouse loyal, honest, good-hearted, committed, dependable, loving? If so, is it really worth getting worked up over a messy toothpaste container?

For Jennifer, dental products are not the issue; it's the hamper. For twelve years, her husband has missed the basket every morning when he tosses his dirty laundry across the room. Does she really believe his aim is that bad? Does she really think that in twelve years he couldn't possibly ever hit the basket—not even one time? Of course not. Yet for Jennifer, it's just not worth the effort to continue bringing it up. Does she have any bad habits her husband has learned to ignore? Let's see. No, she can't think of any offhand. But I'm sure he could tell you a few. For the most part, he's learned to overlook her faults, as she has his. They like to save their disagreements up for the big stuff about once a year—you know, for the things that really matter. Then, after long conversations, sometimes lasting two days, they come to a compromise. Patience. It simply takes patience.

BE PATIENT IN THE PRESENT

Are you always in a hurry to get where you're going? Can't wait for the wedding, your tenth anniversary, your first home, or a new baby? Or are you enjoying this moment, this exact second in time, whether you're planning your nuptials or putting the final details on your fiftieth anniversary party? Remember, you'll be in this place only once. Slow down. Don't hurry. Be patient, and appreciate what you have now. Yes, continue to dream for the future. But take time to enjoy what you already possess. There's no other way to count your blessings than to appreciate what's already in your life.

Do you wonder if your attempts at patience within your relationships go unnoticed by your loved ones and more importantly by God? Scripture shows us that our patience is never in vain:

For God is not unrighteous to forget your work and labour of love, which ye have shewed toward his name, in that ye have ministered to the saints, and do minister. And we desire that every one of you do shew the same diligence to the full assurance of hope unto the end: that ye be not slothful, but followers of them who through faith and patience inherit the promises. For when God made promise to Abraham, because he could swear by no greater, he sware by himself, saying, Surely blessing I will bless thee, and multiplying I will multiply thee. And so, after he had patiently endured, he obtained the promise.

HEBREWS 6:10–15

Many times I've heard young moms shout to their children, "Will you just grow up!" I promise you, they will, in time. In fact, eventually they'll be so grown up that the parents will probably wish they could go back in time, even if only for a moment, to relive those playful childhood moments once more.

Are you still dating? Enjoy the carefree fun. Are you engaged but can't wait for the wedding? Enjoy planning each and every step. Embrace the process rather than the result. It will happen in its time. Are you a newlywed waiting for things to settle down and become smoother? Appreciate this special time of meshing two distinct personalities. Allow the day-to-day change to take place without expecting results overnight. Enjoy the exact moment where God has placed you now. Embrace it. Before you know it, you'll be longing for your close-knit family again, only to discover that you can never recapture its purest essence again. You are making your own family now.

Although solid results from our patient waiting are not always visible, rest assured that in good time they will be noticed, even if only within our own spirit. Scripture assures us:

❧

...If we hope for that we see not, then do we with patience wait for it.

ROMANS 8:25

❧

In time, according to Scripture, good things will come from our patience:

❧

Cast not away therefore your confidence, which hath great recompence of reward. For ye have need of patience, that, after ye have done the will of God, ye might receive the promise.

HEBREWS 10:35–36

KEEP A JOURNAL

A simple tool for embracing patience is to keep a detailed journal. I prefer blank, spiral-bound notebooks, while others like the lovely artistic copies available, with blank pages inside to allow their own free thoughts to come forth.

Whatever your preference, set aside some time each day, or at least once a week, to write down all you appreciate at that very moment. Goal journals are wonderful, but for this particular exercise, use your journal to show appreciation for the present—and therefore practice the virtue of patience.

Be thankful for all you can. Are you healthy? Does your life embrace loved ones? Do you have a home that while perhaps not fully decorated is beautiful in its own way? Are your flowers blooming, even if they're just in a small pot on your apartment deck?

When we journal as such, we discover that although we've been preoccupied with what we lack, we suddenly realize instead all we possess. Life begins to take on an entirely different perspective—instead of wanting, we give thanks; rather than feeling deprived, we feel blessed; in place of our sense of need is a sense of gratitude. When we have a spirit of praise and thanksgiving, we are more in tune with the heart of God than we are at any other moment in our lives.

Now, reflect back upon times of struggle and see where God has taken you. Do you see that through your time and patience, he did work all things out for good? While reflecting upon past burdens that were solved in the end, we can begin to grasp that God knows exactly what he's doing and that therefore, in time, our present concerns will work out for the best, too. We'll finally understand that in God's time, and not a second before, good will come from our burdens, no matter how frustrating they are right now.

Yes, we all have problems to endure and struggles to overcome, but with patience we will work through them. Scripture teaches us how having patience in times of trouble will lead us to a better, more positive life focus:

⁂

…We glory in tribulations also: knowing that tribulation worketh patience; and patience, experience; and experience, hope….

ROMANS 5:3−4

⁂

Although struggles can be stressful, Scripture also teaches us to look at them as a point of growth, in relationships and life in general, assuring us that if we have patience, they will all become blessings:

⁂

My brethren, count it all joy when ye fall into divers temptations; knowing this, that the trying of your faith worketh patience.

But let patience have her perfect work, that ye may be perfect and entire, wanting nothing.

JAMES 1:2–4

❧

As you take quiet moments to thank God for where he's brought you from and to appreciate where you are now, you can begin to let go of anxiety for the future. Leave your burdens prayerfully in his hands and patiently await his answers.

❧

It is a good thing to give thanks unto the LORD,
And to sing praises unto thy name, O most High:
To shew forth thy lovingkindness in the morning,
And thy faithfulness every night,
Upon an instrument of ten strings, and upon the psaltery;
Upon the harp with a solemn sound.
For thou, LORD, hast made me glad through thy work:
I will triumph in the works of thy hands.
O LORD, how great are thy works!
And thy thoughts are very deep.

PSALM 92:1–5

❧

Over the years, I've found the following to be particularly helpful: When I'm in times of doubt, I look back on my complete history of answered prayer, of personal situations that worked out for the better, and of hope born anew, and I realize that placing my future, my life, and my marriage in God's hands is the ultimate foundation of security.

By journaling your gratitude, you will find less pressure on your marriage to achieve instant perfection and more appreciation in your heart instead of anxiety. Before you know it, a spirit of gratitude will take hold of your household, and peace and patience will prevail.

Scripture teaches us the benefit of praise:

Praise ye the LORD.
Sing unto the LORD a new song,
And his praise in the congregation of saints.
Let Israel rejoice in him that made him:
Let the children of Zion be joyful in their King.
Let them praise his name in the dance:
let them sing praises unto him with the timbrel and harp.
For the LORD taketh pleasure in his people:
He will beautify the meek with salvation.

Let the saints be joyful in glory:
Let them sing aloud upon their beds.
Let the high praises of God be in their mouth....

❧

❦ TIPS TO TAKE AWAY ❦

§ *Don't hurry love.* Make careful, slow decisions. Consider all your life experience when choosing a forever partner. Prayerfully listen to your inner voice—often known as the still, small voice of God. Rather than making a fast, quick, "now or never" decision, grasp the importance of your choice and its dramatic impact on your life, and prayerfully weigh all your options.

§ *Be patient with your loved one.* We must give others the freedom to grow. Feel free to encourage your spouse's growth, but don't stand by with a measuring stick each morning to see if your expectations have been met. Encouragement and patience will prompt more change than angry accusations ever will.

¶ *Be patient with yourself.* We're all learning, and that means you, too. Set your goals, be realistic about what truly needs adjusting, and then begin to move prayerfully forward. Don't demand change in yourself overnight. Trees take time to bear fruit; so do we.

¶ *Be patient for your dreams.* Enjoy the present. Embrace the moment. Feed your dreams, as an individual and a couple, but wait for those dreams with patient grace instead of anxious expectations. In time, if they are meant to happen, they will. Remember, patience is the key to joy in the now.

¶ *Be patient with differences.* Make a list, mental or literal, of things you and your partner disagree about, and decide which of them really matter. If something won't really make a difference in the long run, quickly remove it from your agenda and from your mind. But if it does truly matter, address that point, weigh it out, and come to a mutual compromise. Understand what your personal deal breakers are; then stick to your moral self. But also understand what changes are workable within your relationship, and be patient as they slowly come to fruition.

¶ *Be patient in the present.* Live your life for the moment, not for what it might become later. Experience it, appreciate it, take note of it, pay attention to it, and count every blessing.

II.

LOVE IS KIND

Gentleness and a kind spirit are signs of a spiritually giving individual, one whose relationships depend on such high-caliber character. In a world filled with hurried, it's-all-about-me individuals, one rarely gets the opportunity to breathe in kindness in its purest form. And yet we all crave it instinctively and are drawn closer by its flavor.

CHOOSE A KIND MATE

Consider it a priority to make a wise, spiritually guided choice about the man you plan to spend the rest of your life with. If you start out with the right person, the odds of success are clearly stacked in your favor.

Love is composed of a single soul inhabiting two bodies.

ARISTOTLE

Although you may believe the best test of your fiancé's character is simply to gauge how you're being treated, you can sometimes learn more about him by watching how he behaves toward others.

Several years ago, Karen was dating an attractive, older, divorced man. He treated her exceptionally well. The two seemed happy and began contemplating marriage.

One day, she told her friends that the man she was madly in love with had little to no contact with his grown children. In fact, for most of their childhood, he rarely saw them at all. Sensing her friends' concern, she tried to explain the situation further. Apparently, his wife had passed away when the kids were quite young. Not knowing what to do, he dropped them off with their grandmother, proceeded to move on with his life, and took a rather hands-off attitude toward the entire child-rearing process—both financially and emotionally.

Karen's friends tried to suggest gently that his lack of loyalty would eventually come back to bite her. Unfortunately, she doubted them completely. After all, she insisted, the man treated her like gold. Why should she care what kind of father he'd been over the years? Since Karen no longer had young ones at home, she just couldn't see how this man's parenting commitment, or lack thereof, impacted their adult relationship at all. Her wise friends' response? Pay attention to the details around you, because character is everything.

In time, and just shortly into the couple's engagement, Karen's boyfriend's selfishness and clear lack of loyalty was revealed when he was caught red-handed cheating on her. Although she was saddened by her difficult ordeal, Karen was glad she discovered the truth in time—before the wedding.

Character counts. If your fiancé treats you well but is disloyal to others, you'd better prepare yourself for the inevitable. Instead of turning a blind eye to the obvious, prayerfully ask God to show you the truth. Then watch, listen, and continue to pray for divine guidance. No matter what, be aware that character really is everything.

PRACTICE THE GOLDEN RULE

How often do you look at the Golden Rule as something you do for strangers, your neighbors, or coworkers but not necessarily for your spouse? Yet there is perhaps no higher calling than to treat your loved one the way you would like to be treated.

❧

If you want to be loved, be lovable.

OVID

❧

God himself teaches us through Scripture that our truest heart is revealed through acts of loving-kindness:

❧

A new commandment I give unto you, That ye love one another;
as I have loved you, that ye also love one another. By this shall all men
know that ye are my disciples, if ye have love one to another.

JOHN 13:34–35

❧

Remember, God commands us to love. Kindness is an extension of a loving spirit. Throughout this lifetime, we will be known by our fruitful actions.

❧

Herein is my Father glorified, that ye bear much fruit; so shall ye be my disciples. As the Father hath loved me, so have I loved you: continue ye in my love. If ye keep my commandments, ye shall abide in my love; even as I have kept my Father's commandments, and abide in his love.

These things have I spoken unto you, that my joy might remain in you, and that your joy might be full. This is my commandment, That ye love one another, as I have loved you.

JOHN 15:8-12

❧

Hopefully, since our own terrible twos, we've learned that the world doesn't completely revolve around us. Most likely, we've grown enough and begun to grasp the fact that to receive, we must first lovingly give. To have caring relationships, it's essential that we put kindness, and others' feelings, in the forefront of our lives.

Unfortunately, when it comes to kindness, many of us are guilty of treating strangers with more dignity than we give our closest loved ones.

And we often pay the price for such behavior. Perhaps we act this way because we feel our spouses will be the first ones to accept our harsh attitude. If we're frustrated and take anger out on our loved ones, it's probably because we feel their toleration level is perhaps higher than that of our boss or the clerk at the local grocery store. I'm afraid that after the dating is over and the wedding rings are on, polished up and gleaming brightly, many of us believe our mates will put up with resounding negativity. How sad.

I must admit, on occasion I've been guilty myself. I remember one particular afternoon when my day had been extremely harried. My kids and I had just arrived home, and we were expecting a dozen or so 4-H children to knock on our door in less than 45 minutes. One quick look around the house told me that we needed to do some serious cleaning, and we needed to do it fast. So I asked my teen daughter, Tiffany, to quickly scrub the sink with cleanser. Her reply? "I don't know how to use cleanser."

Okay, go ahead and get it out of your system—let out that big sigh. Sure, by now she should have known how to perform such a simple task. But stay with me for a moment while I reveal more. My reaction, rather than a quick explanation, went far beyond the necessary. Frustrated by the hectic nature of my day and the fact that we had only minutes to get the house into shape, I began to yell—loudly: "What do you mean you don't know how to clean the sink? You pour in the cleanser, wipe it out with a sponge, and rinse it down the drain! This is not rocket science!"

It wasn't my words, mind you, that I regret in the least. It was my tone, which clearly displayed I was out of control. In fact, the entire time I was yelling, I remember thinking, "Candy, you're completely over-the-top here. Get a grip. You'd never shout at anyone else this way." But deep down inside, I have to admit that I was going for the drama that only some heavy-duty yelling might get across.

Then, just as I was shifting into high gear, I was stopped by the ringing of the doorbell. You guessed it—time for a bit of heavenly motivated humiliation. When I opened the door, I discovered my neighbor, who had innocently stopped by to ask a brief question. Needless to say, I was mortified! I was caught red-handed being a rude jerk. My neighbor politely said nothing about my dramatic scene, but I have no doubt that she heard it. In fact, I'm convinced to this day that she probably ran right home and said to her husband, "Wow, you should have heard that inspirational author next door yelling like a maniac." Yep, I was caught, and I definitely deserved it.

Afterward, I took a moment, settled down, and apologized to my daughter (who, by the way, found the entire episode wildly amusing). It was a humbling experience for me, and it was, I believe, orchestrated by God. It taught me a great lesson about always treating my loved ones, whether my closest friends, my children, or my spouse, with the same, kindness, respect, and dignity I'd gladly offer a stranger.

❧

Love is not something you feel. It's something you do.

DAVID WILKERSON

❧

In Scripture, God teaches us to fight fairly. He clearly warns us numerous times to avoid unnecessary strife:

❧

The mouth of a righteous man is a well of life:
But violence covereth the mouth of the wicked.
Hatred stirreth up strifes:
But love covereth all sins.

PROVERBS 10:11‒12

❧

Scripture even teaches us that unkind words may never be forgotten:

❧

A brother offended is harder to be won than a strong city:
And their contentions are like the bars of a castle.

PROVERBS 18:19

❧

We must, therefore, treat each other with loving-kindness, because God is our inspiration:

❧

Beloved, let us love one another: for love is of God; and every one that loveth is born of God, and knoweth God. He that loveth not, knoweth not God; for God is love.

1 JOHN 4:7–8

❧

So what does this have to do with marriage, you might ask? Well, I've been around enough to know that the way we talk to our kids is typically the way we talk to our spouses. We don't always offer them our best jewels of inspiration. Treat your spouse and all your loved ones as you would have them treat you.

After the wedding and, obviously, the dating are over, there's absolutely no reason to set aside your best attitude. Yes, you need to be real, but why should the acts of kindness stop—opening a car door, sending flowers, baking your husband's favorite cookies, offering gentle, encouraging words at just the right moment? Yet I'm sure you're aware that for many people in this world, they unfortunately do.

In the mid-1980s, when I was dating my husband, he was the only man who had ever brought me flowers. On our first date, he arrived with a single red rose. I thanked him and then quietly placed it in a vase. I casually pretended that receiving a rose was an everyday occurrence, but deep down inside, I was shouting, Yes, he brought me flowers!

Months later, and well into our engagement, when the blossoms continued to arrive, a future in-law took me aside and decided to rain on my parade. "Enjoy this treatment now, "she said, "because the second you get married, you'll never receive flowers again. Trust me. Men are all alike."

Call me naive, but I was taken aback by her bold statement. After all, I thought it was simply part of Patrick's kind personality and never believed for a moment that it might be nothing more than clever dating strategy. So I immediately brought it to his attention. "Is this true?" I asked. "Will you really stop bringing me bouquets as soon as we're married?" Patrick looked at me with sincerity and said, "I'll always bring you flowers, honey."

This may surprise you, but guess what? I believed him. And you know, to this very day, more than seventeen years later, he's been good to his word. Patrick obviously understood that simple kindness will be appreciated even many years after the wedding.

BE OPEN TO RECEIVING AS WELL AS GIVING

Although most people love to receive and on occasion struggle with giving, some, like myself, have more difficulty being the receiver of another's kindness. If you're one of these individuals, look deep into your soul and attempt to discover what it is that keeps you from being blessed by others. Do you feel unworthy? Do you shudder at the thought of putting another person out? Do you see yourself only in the role of giver, and never as receiver?

Over the years, I've learned that other people get as much joy from giving as I do. When I deny their spiritual blessing because it makes me uncomfortable, I've denied them the simple joy of offering their best.

As I write this chapter, Janet, my neighbor, is preparing to entertain eighteen people in her home for dinner. Yes, you read that right—eighteen. Putting aside the fact that she must be nuts, let's take a look at how she handled the food arrangements. Each and every invited couple has asked her repeatedly what they can bring to the table. And each and every time, Janet's firmly replied, "Please don't bring a thing—I've got it all covered." Finally, after I made many requests, she gave in. "If you really want to contribute something," she said, "you can bring a bottle of your favorite wine." Oddly enough, I'd like you to know, this simple compromise nearly put her out of commission. She thought about it and anguished over it for days.

At last, Janet had to ask herself why she was having so much difficulty being blessed by others. After all, when she goes to her neighbor's home, she never hesitates to bring something along to share. She does it for the simple reason that she enjoys giving. Janet understands that giving to others is part of the human experience. Yet her first instinct when others offer to give in return is to block them from reciprocating.

Two other acquaintances of mine provide another example of this situation. A couple years ago, Marla's friend Cara landed a fantastic job. Yet when the two meet for lunch, Marla's willing to pay for Cara, but she never allows her friend to reciprocate. When Cara offers, even if it's just to purchase a cup of coffee, Marla goes off the deep end, acting out in a tizzy. Cara often gives her a reality check by jokingly remarking, "Marla, get a grip. It's just a cup of coffee. Remember…" she tells her, "I'm your rich friend; I can afford the two bucks." Her humorous words quickly put things into perspective, but to this day, even on Marla's birthday, Cara's never allowed to make good on her offer. Isn't that silly?

On a similar note, several years ago, my husband purchased a special sapphire-and-diamond ring for my birthday. It was beautiful, and I was amazed at the good taste and thought it took to find it. The following year,

Patrick joyfully purchased a beautiful pair of diamond earrings from the same store. Now, here's where my inability to receive came into play. Although the earrings were lovely, they clearly were not your everyday accessory. Due to their price, which I determined was more than we could afford, and the fact that I could wear them only on specialoccasions, I decided I couldn't accept the gift. My husband was obviously disappointed by my reaction, but I insisted, thinking I was doing the right thing.

In case you're wondering, yes, I was grateful. Yes, I appreciated his romantic thoughtfulness and the kind gesture it represented, but my practical side just determined I simply wasn't worthy of a gift that could only be worn a couple times a year. Really, what were the odds I was going to be invited to the Academy Awards? So, much to my husband's dismay, I went back to the store to exchange it for something more practical. I decided upon a bracelet that I thought could be worn daily, but in fact, I still feel it is too dressy, so sadly it sits, wasting away in my dresser drawer.

When I arrived back at the jewelry department, the salesclerk on duty offered me a great lesson. I only wish her message had soaked in then, and not years after the fact. Without a doubt, she thought I was doing the wrong thing by returning a special, romantic gift from my husband, and let me tell you, she made no attempt to hide her feelings. In reality, was it any of her business? Of course not. Was she out of line by lecturing me? You betcha. Was she, in fact, worried about her reduction in commission?

(The bracelet cost less.) Probably so. However, even taking all that into consideration, I must admit now that her words were right on target.

"You know, I rarely see men surprise their wives with jewelry," she said. "Most of the time, the women pick the item out and then the spouses reluctantly go along with the purchase. But your husband came in proud of his idea, thrilled with his choice, and clearly wanting to please you. Don't you realize that by exchanging this gift, you're going to hurt his feelings? I promise you, if you make this exchange, he'll never buy you jewelry again."

That lecture may be hard for you to believe, but I promise, it happened. I bit my lip and controlled myself from letting her know my marriage was none of her business. Then, feeling a need to defend my actions, I tried, once again, to explain my motives. After all, I was simply attempting to save my husband money on a gift I'd hardly be able to use. How often does the typical woman take care of the kids, go on walks with the neighbors, or write books while wearing dangling diamond earrings?

After the clerk was sure she couldn't change my mind, she reluctantly exchanged my purchase, and I walked out of the store sure I'd done the right thing. Looking back, I realize that her words made a great deal of sense. And true to her prediction, my husband has never again bought me a piece of jewelry. But most of all, I realize now that by questioning my value as the receiver, I hurt the giver in the process. Kindness can be fulfilled only if the recipient is willing to accept the gift without question.

For many of us, not only material objects but also simple words of kindness bring our insecurities into play. Has someone ever complimented your outfit, only to be met with words like, "Oh, this old thing? I bought it for a dollar from my neighbor's garage sale." Or worse yet, "You're kidding. These pants make my rear look enormous!" My friend Lisa often tells me, "Candy, just say 'thank you' and move on. Quit knocking yourself. Learn to graciously accept compliments as nothing more than the kindnesses they were intended to be."

When Sue had her portrait taken, she offered a wallet-size copy to her husband. He liked it so much that he asked for a larger print so he could have it framed and place it on his office desk. Not knowing how to handle the obvious compliment, Sue jokingly replied, "Yikes, look at the lines under my eyes in that picture! If you put it on your desk, why don't you add a little donation cup for my future face-lift fund, so your coworkers can throw a dime in every time they walk by." But instead of laughing, her husband simply said, "Now I'm not sure if I even want the picture anymore. Why do you do that? Why do you have to make every compliment I offer into a joke?" Realizing she had been ungracious in her reply, Sue tried to explain she was only kidding and practically pushed the photo back in her husband's direction. He did take it to work as planned, but Sue realized that if she was able to give in kindness, she must be willing to receive as well.

So, if you're a giver but can't see yourself on the receiving end, look into your heart and search your soul. Try to remember that whether you are offered the kindness of a stranger, a gift from your best friend, or a genuine blessing from your partner, you should graciously enjoy it and just say "thank you" rather than pushing it away, feeling you're at all unworthy.

CREATE A SAFE HAVEN

We all need a haven to come to after struggling in what can sometimes be a rough and offensive world. Whether we've been working, volunteering, or just battling it out in traffic, we all desire a place where peace and kindness reign. This is the very least we should expect from our relationships.

By filling our home with kindness, making it a no-war zone, we are blessing everyone who enters our door. Our children, spouses, friends, and neighbors will feel a sense of peace as they're embraced by the spirit of our household.

❧

Little deeds of kindness, little words of love,
Help to make earth happy like the heaven above.

JULIA A. FLETCHER CARNEY

❧

Providing a place of refuge from the storms of life is also essential for a peaceful personal existence. Who wants to come home from intense battles on the work front, only to fight it out with those we love? Wouldn't we all prefer to spend time with a spouse who cares enough to offer kind words, encouragement, and blessing? Bring joy, peace, and loving-kindness to your marriage, your home, and your family, and provide a sacred place of escape from what's often a hard and troublesome world.

ARGUE FAIRLY

Does creating a safe haven mean we can never argue? Gosh, I hope not, or I'm way off track. Of course we all have disagreements. This is a real world, and with real relationships, there will be real problems. Yet there are ways to handle conflicts with kindness, without allowing them to turn into ugly, painful, all-out wars.

First, decide what your deal breakers are. Each of us has a short list of what we will, and will not, tolerate from anyone. No one deserves abuse, either physical or emotional. No one. Once you know that, and your spouse does too, you're way ahead of many folks.

However, most disagreements in life are about the inconsequential stuff, such as who drove the kids to soccer last time, and why in the world is it my turn to bring them again? Or who's going to do the dishes tonight, and why does my spouse insist on using fourteen glasses per day? How about, who went over the budget—again? These situations clearly warrant discussions, but be sure to validate your points with kindness. Yelling, screaming, and worse yet, name-calling, will only place you in a horrible situation for negotiations, respect, and any chance at future communication. In essence, you've lost the battle before you've even begun.

I'm still shocked at how many friends have confided in me that in the midst of arguments, their husbands stoop to calling them horrible names. And yes, I'm sure there are women out there who do the same. Obviously, emotional abuse is not the way to instill change in your spouse. It's nothing more than an attempt to belittle someone into desperate submission.

Trust me, I've had my fair share of arguments with my husband over the years, but never (no, not ever) have we resorted to name-calling. I've never said, "Well, you're stupid….," and he's never replied, "You're lazy…." Why? Because after the argument is over, I promise you, we'd remember those words FOREVER. That's precisely how unfair fighting backfires.

I have friends who are still steamed that three years ago in the heat of arguing, their spouses said terrible things such as "You're fat" and "I wish I never married you in the first place." Let me tell you, when a disagreement like that is over, you can apologize until the cows come home—you can swear you didn't really mean it and that it was all said simply in the heat of anger—but believe me on this one, your spouse will remember forever each and every last word you uttered. Yes, what we say can cut deeply, and the wounds that we inflict can be permanent. So guard your words and actions, covering them with kindness. Arguments come and go, but a cruel spirit is remembered always.

Scripture teaches us that our actions of kindness and our loving attitudes are profitable to our world, our relationships, and our marriages:

A merry heart maketh a cheerful countenance:
But by sorrow of the heart the spirit is broken.
The heart of him that hath understanding seeketh knowledge:
But the mouth of fools feedeth on foolishness.
All the days of the afflicted are evil:
But he that is of a merry heart hath a continual feast.
Better is little with the fear of the LORD
Than great treasure with trouble therewith.
Better is a dinner of herbs where love is,
Than a stalled ox and hatred therewith.
A wrathful man stirreth up strife:
But he that is slow to anger appeaseth strife.

PROVERBS 15:13–18

INITIATE SMALL ACTS OF KINDNESS

Sometimes it's the little things we remember most. I can recall in detail the times I came home from elementary school, soaking wet from the rain, and my mom was waiting for me with hot cocoa, warm, dry clothes, and a tender hug. I can still smell the hot chocolate simmering on the stove; I can feel her sweet embrace. And I can experience a distinct feeling of peace when I relive her kindness, even after all of these years.

God requires us to base our actions in loving-kindness. In this way, we fulfill his commandments.

❧

Owe no man any thing, but to love one another: for he that loveth another hath fulfilled the law. For this, Thou shalt not commit adultery, Thou shalt not kill, Thou shalt not steal, Thou shalt not bear false witness, Thou shalt not covet; and if there be any other commandment, it is briefly comprehended in this saying, namely, Thou shalt love thy neighbour as thyself. Love worketh no ill to his neighbour: therefore love is the fulfilling of the law.

ROMANS 13:8–10

❧

We may claim to have faith, but if our hearts are not full of love and our actions are not filled with kindness, Scripture says, the truth about us is revealed:

※

And we have known and believed the love that God hath to us. God is love; and he that dwelleth in love dwelleth in God, and God in him. Herein is our love made perfect, that we may have boldness in the day of judgment: because as he is, so are we in this world. There is no fear in love; but perfect love casteth out fear: because fear hath torment. He that feareth is not made perfect in love. We love him, because he first loved us. If a man say, I love God, and hateth his brother, he is a liar: for he that loveth not his brother whom he hath seen, how can he love God whom he hath not seen? And this commandment have we from him. That he who loveth God love his brother also.

1 JOHN 4:16–21

※

We can help to make positive permanent memories for our loved ones and others around us, and sometimes it's with the littlest things. How much effort is it to make your spouse's favorite meal, bring flowers in from the garden, surprise him with breakfast in bed, wash his car, or just offer an encouraging word at the right moment? I promise, these little things will be remembered for a lifetime and will make your marriage, your home life, and your relationships a lot smoother and more caring than they'd be if you stayed in your own self-absorbed world.

DON'T EXPECT TO GET EXACTLY WHAT YOU WANT

My husband is a wonderful cook. He prepares fantastic meals with great finesse, making sure each bite is a delectable morsel. Then he presents the food with beauty and grace (no throwing side dishes haphazardly on a plate for this guy). On special occasions, he even sets the table beautifully. Wow, sounds too good to be true, you say? Well, hold on, because I'm not finished yet. When Patrick cooks, he does not exactly, shall I say, clean up as he goes along. So each time he prepares a grand meal, the kitchen is filled with every utensil, every pan, and every mixing bowl this side of the Food Network. In fact, knowing full well that he doesn't plan to pick up, he tends to use more dishes than your average cook would ever dream of.

There have been times when I've walked into the dining room to see a gorgeous table setting and food presentation that would make the owner of a five-star restaurant red with envy, only to be told the following: "Whatever you do, honey, don't go into the kitchen!" Anyway, I've learned to appreciate my husband's acts of kindness even if they're not always the gifts I'd like to receive. I could complain; however, I take great pleasure in appreciating the gifts he offers. I'd rather concentrate on the positive and count my blessings than complain about a sauce-splattered kitchen any day.

❧

That best portion of a good man's life—
His little, nameless, unremembered acts
Of kindness and of love.

WILLIAM WORDSWORTH

❧

Although we all know it's true, we often forget that no one is perfect. So instead of expecting perfection, be grateful for your spouse's good intentions, and learn to work out the concerns that you honestly feel need to be addressed. Be open to small acts of kindness even if they don't come with all the bells and whistles you had hoped for.

❧ TIPS TO TAKE AWAY ❧

¶ *Choose a kind mate.* Instead of attempting to fix endless problems after you're married, make it your priority to ask for divine wisdom about your chosen partner before the wedding. Always ask for, listen to, and then act upon the instructions from that still, small voice dwelling within you.

§ *Practice the Golden Rule.* Once you are married, by all means, treat your husband as well as, if not better than, you do others. After all, why should he be treated any less? Although we often think our loved ones must put up with more, the reality is, they don't have to, nor should they. Before you take your tension out on your spouse, remember his place in your world and your desire to create a blessed relationship. Then act in kindness.

§ *Be kind even after the wedding.* Don't forget to treat your husband with the same love and respect you did while you were dating. Just because you're married is no reason to slack off now. Continue to present the kind heart and gentle spirit that drew you to each other in the first place. Think of your marriage in terms of your early relationship and see it improve.

§ *Be open to receiving as well as giving.* If you struggle with receiving but are free with your giving personality, search your soul and ask your Creator for the ability to graciously receive the blessings and kindness that others willingly offer, whether it's a compliment or a simple, or even extravagant, material gift. Never let your own insecurities cause you to unwillingly stifle another from the simple joy of giving.

¶ *Create a safe haven.* Don't allow your home to become a war zone. Make it a place of kindness, where you can both go to get away from a sometimes cruel and chaotic world.

¶ *Argue fairly.* Remember kindness even in the midst of a disagreement. This is not the time to say things you don't mean just to get a reaction or push the other into submission. All the apologies in the world won't make up for those unkind words once the fight is over.

¶ *Initiate small acts of kindness.* It doesn't take much. Did you used to cook your husband's favorite meal and serve it up by candlelight? Then why stop now? How about offering to watch his favorite show or rent his favorite movie? Or give him a card just to say "I love you." Simple gestures will be remembered for a lifetime. You'll be surprised.

¶ *Don't expect to get exactly what you want.* Remember to accept the kindness even when it comes in different avenues than you expected. Rather than questioning the gift because it doesn't fit the mold you anticipated, be grateful and appreciative. By doing so, you'll encourage the positive gestures and will insure that kind, loving behavior will continue long into the future.

III.

Love Is Not Envious

Scripture teaches us that love is not envious. In reality, true love enables you to support your partner even if it looks as though the fulfillment of his dreams may have surpassed your own. Clearly, there's no room for envy in a loving marriage. So instead of filling your heart with strife, propelled by a spirit of jealousy, fill it with genuine joy for one another's success, never allowing envy or the fear of being left behind to come between you.

CONFESS YOUR ENVY

Do you fear your husband's success may change him so immensely that he will no longer want to be with you? If you suspect this might be the case, sit down in a quiet place, ask yourself some serious questions, take a peek into your soul, and begin to address your fears.

What kind of questions should you ask? First, ask yourself where these fears come from. From what level of insecurity do they arise? Then begin to pray for guidance, for revelation about your own motives, and for the ability to face and defeat your doubts. Ask God to reveal your envy and to help you replace your fears with peace, offering a supportive heart instead of one filled with destructive jealousy.

One of the ten commandments teaches us that we should not allow envy to create a covetous spirit:

❧

Thou shalt not covet thy neighbour's house, thou shalt not covet thy neighbour's wife, nor his manservant, nor his maidservant, nor his ox, nor his ass, nor any thing that is thy neighbour's.

EXODUS 20:17

❧

Scripture also teaches us that there's more to life than material blessings. Envy and covetousness are not part of God's plan for our lives.

❧

And he said unto them, Take heed, and beware of covetousness: for a man's life consisteth not in the abundance of the things which he possesseth.

❧

Once you've gone inside yourself and asked God for guidance and redirection, consider expressing your envy out loud. Sure, it can be embarrassing, but once it's out in the open, things often fall into perspective.

Many years ago, I sat in a car with my friend Lisa. Just a few months before, she had inherited a substantial amount of money. Although I was happy for her good fortune, there was a part of me that was grappling with envy. Although I had previously thought it through and prayed about it, strange feelings, ever so subtle, were definitely there. So that day in the car, I whispered to her, "You know, Lisa, this is horrible to admit, but there's a small part of me that, quite frankly, is a bit envious of your wealth. I don't like it, but I want you to know that's how I feel."

Love Is Not Envious 65

Did my friend react in horror? Did she open the car door and throw me out? Did she refuse to speak to me ever again, nullifying our years of rock-solid friendship? No. In fact, quite the opposite was true. Lisa simply smiled knowingly and said, "Candy, I'm so glad you confessed what you were feeling. You know, it's pretty obvious to me that many of my other friends feel that way too, but no one else will admit it to my face. I'm glad you brought it out into the open. We can work it out." And guess what? After that brief moment of admission, there was no reason to work through anything. In my case, the envy in my spirit ended right then and there. I had prayed about it. I had confessed my sin to my friend, and thankfully, she understood. Much to my pleasure, the envy never returned again.

BE SUPPORTIVE

Does your husband have dreams that require him to shoot for the moon? Are you fearful that such success may change the very fabric of your marriage? Human nature can often bring out the spirit of envy even among those we love. Yet because we've taken a vow to cherish our spouses and support them through thick and thin, we must set aside those fears, analyze where they come from, and deal with them directly. Perhaps your spouse wants to fulfill a dream career or has lofty goals to travel worldwide. Perhaps these are not your dreams. But instead of popping his bubble and offering every reason why he shouldn't pursue his goals, why not encourage him and help him fulfill his dreams? In that way, you'll reveal a loving spirit, one that isn't envious of your husband's potential blessings but that rejoices in his good, even above your own.

Fortunately, most of us do not have spouses whose jobs might easily invoke attacks of jealousy. Let's say your husband were an actor. Can you imagine how uncomfortable it would be to send him off to work, knowing that by noon, he'd be filming a love scene with a gorgeous, nearly perfect creature? Okay, I get it. It's a job. Uh-huh, you betcha, I understand—no personal feelings involved. It's only acting. But I just have to ask: Could you deal with it? Well, me neither. Yet there are folks who struggle with these issues every day, and if they love their partners, they somehow manage to work them out. Thank goodness most of us simply need to support dreams and goals that better our spouses but will never require them to smooch it up with strangers from 9 to 5 just to bring home the bacon. What else can I say but count your blessings!

There are practical ways to actively defeat envy. Rather than emotionally sabotaging your relationship, you can go the extra mile and actively help each other's dreams to come true. Consider asking your husband to pick up the household slack while you take a writing course, oil-painting classes, or singing lessons. Maybe you can hold down the fort for a few years while he goes back to school and tackles the combination of home life and classroom. Instead of being envious that he has an opportunity to fulfill his dreams, and wondering how much that will put you in perceived jeopardy, reach out, support, and encourage his successful blessings.

DON'T COMPETE WITH YOUR SPOUSE

Have you ever seen anything more pathetic than a husband and wife competing with each other? Whether they're in the job world or just trying to grab the attention at a party because they're feeling a bit slighted, their display of envy is never pretty.

There'll be times when your husband's star seems to rise above your own, but don't let envy get a grip on your heart. Instead, rejoice. Your day will also come. There will be times when your star will shine, and you should expect the same joyous response from those who love you. Anything less demonstrates a selfish and nonsupportive spirit.

≥≤

Love is a fruit in season at all times, and within reach of every hand.

MOTHER TERESA

≥≤

I'm sure you've seen aging fathers compete with their youthful sons out of jealousy. How about mothers who compete with their daughters for attention? If your loved one has been lucky enough to achieve a prominent social status or a place in the spotlight, be gracious and supportive of his success. Yes, strive for your own, but do it with grace and with genuine joy for your husband's blessings. After all, you do love him and want the very best for his life, right?

THROW OUT THE GREEN-EYED MONSTER

When envy goes beyond wishing you could have what another has to wanting to take it away, you've crossed the line into full-blown jealousy. If you're with someone who has such deep inner fears and intense insecurities that they see a threat around every corner to the very existence of your relationship, address the problem immediately. Such jealousy can be an early sign of unacceptable, and possibly dangerous, control.

But unless there is a history of untrustworthy behavior, believing in your spouse is essential to the blessing of marriage. Never allow jealousy to take hold of your relationship. Talk over your fears with each other and God. If those feelings are not founded in reality but are simply the spirit of jealousy, based on your own insecurities, put your heart and relationship into God's hands and begin to thrive again.

Of course, love requires you to give no reason for a fair-minded person to become jealous. If you're intentionally doing something that makes your spouse uncomfortable, then you must ask yourself if your freedom to do so is worth hurting the one you love. It's important to know the difference between unreasonable insecurity and insecurity founded in fairness. Does your spouse want to keep you away from family, from friends, or from anyone he sees as a threat to your relationship? Then get help fast. You are not dealing with someone who has your best interest at heart, but with an individual whose sole purpose is control.

However, if your husband is uncomfortable with the level of a certain friendship you have with someone else and he feels it's causing a distance between you, then prayerfully talk it over, and consider ending that contact for the good of your marriage. In the end, making sure your spouse is feeling at peace with your relationship is far more important than the freedom to associate with everyone you please.

My friend Teri was working late one night when a group of coworkers decided to end the evening by going dancing. She declined to go along. One young man said, "I guess your husband wouldn't want you to go dancing without him." Without hesitation, Teri quickly replied, "Actually, I just know I wouldn't appreciate him going dancing after midnight without me. So I wouldn't want to put him in the same uncomfortable position." Teri didn't need to think about it. She just knew it wasn't worth hurting her husband's feelings.

Now, I know there are couples who love to dance, and some spouses have no problem if their partners go out without them to enjoy their hobby.

That's not my point. However, it's important to evaluate your own personality, decide what is acceptable to you and what blesses and detracts your marriage, and go from there. You'll know in your spirit when an action is inappropriate and when it's just good, healthy fun. Never tolerate unfounded jealousy or rage, but never encourage jealousy because you're flaunting your freedom at the risk of hurting the one you love.

On occasion, jealousy can be a healthy sign or warning. Always listen to your instincts. Lynette was shocked when her husband of twenty years ran off with someone he'd recently met on the Internet. I know what you're thinking; in fact, I can almost hear you groaning now. Her hubby occupied his days off on the computer while Lynette was busy working as a grocery checkout clerk just a few miles from their home. What had started out innocently as surfing the Net and meeting new friends in chat rooms unfortunately ended in devastation.

Here's where legitimate jealousy came into play. When Lynette told her husband she was uncomfortable with him spending so much time in chat rooms, he brushed her off with accusations that she was being insecure and petty. He insisted he hadn't done anything wrong and that she needed to deal with her issues. Yet in the end, her instincts proved to be right. Isn't that usually the case? I can't help but agree with the age-old wisdom—never doubt a woman's intuition. Sure enough, within a few months, this online-addicted husband asked Lynette for a divorce, claiming he was in love with a woman he'd never even met! Their marriage is now over, and their two teenagers live without a father because of his horrible choices and unwillingness to let go of his freedom when his spouse said she was extremely uncomfortable.

A few years ago, an acquaintance told me that she and her husband abided by the following policy: "We can flirt all we want," she said, "but we can't touch." Let me tell you, boy did they! Their public displays were merciless: Whatever one started, the other tried to outdo, and each fed into the other's jealousy, hoping to come out on top. Did their desperate attempt for attention work? Yes. But did it get them the results they were looking for? I don't think so. The couple has since broken up. Is anyone really surprised?

Scripture teaches us to be different from unbelievers. We may have lived a life filled with envy and strife, but God has a better plan.

⚶

...Speak evil of no man, to be no brawlers, but gentle, shewing all meekness unto all men. For we ourselves also were sometimes foolish, disobedient, deceived, serving divers lusts and pleasures, living in malice and envy, hateful, and hating one another. But after that the kindness and love of God our Saviour toward man appeared, not by works of righteousness which we have done, but according to his mercy he saved us, by the washing of regeneration, and renewing of the Holy Ghost;

which he shed on us abundantly through Jesus Christ our Saviour; that being justified by his grace, we should be made heirs according to the hope of eternal life. This is a faithful saying, and these things I will that thou affirm constantly, that they which have believed in God might be careful to maintain good works. These things are good and profitable unto men. But avoid foolish questions, and genealogies, and contentions, and strivings about the law; for they are unprofitable and vain.

TITUS 3:2–9

❧

DON'T FEED ENVY

Have you ever been around someone who bragged endlessly? Did it make you want to yawn, tune them out, or just pick up your belongings and run screaming for the hills? If you said yes to any or all of the above, trust me— you're not alone. Nobody wants to be around people who flaunt what they have, who they are, or what they've done. In essence, these people are simply attempting to instill a spirit of envy within you for their own selfish purposes.

Several months ago, a group of friends met for dinner. During the course of the evening, one gentleman mentioned at every opportunity possible that he was a doctor. Now, I want you to understand, this was no surprise to anyone in the room. They all knew he was a doctor; in fact, they were even familiar with the specific type of medicine he practices. Yet this man managed to work his job title into the conversation even when it made no sense to do so at all.

When the party finally ended, the hostess asked her husband what he thought. Not usually one to overanalyze people's ulterior motives, he quickly replied, "Guess what? That doctor won't be spending another evening with us anytime soon." And by the way, he hasn't.

Do I understand this man's motivation? Actually, I do. Sometimes, due to a lack of self-esteem, we attempt to flaunt ourselves in order to draw out the spirit of envy in others. One evening, while entertaining friends, my husband was asked about his job. He immediately downplayed many of his responsibilities. The others specifically asked about a new contract he was overseeing, and to hear Patrick tell it, he did absolutely nothing all day long except stare aimlessly out the window. Of course, looking back, I realize he was just being graciously modest.

However, when everyone left, I asked Patrick why he had not expressed what he did for a living in a more positive light. "Why should I do that, Candy," he said. "I know who I am. I don't need to impress anyone." Ouch! When he's right, he's right. Clearly, it wasn't necessary for my husband to invoke a spirit of envy in others just to feel good about himself.

We can ask God for help with an envious spirit. If we draw close to him, he will free us from our struggle to compete in unhealthy ways.

❧

Do ye think that the scripture saith in vain, The spirit that dwelleth in us lusteth to envy? But he giveth more grace. Wherefore he saith, God resisteth the proud, but giveth grace unto the humble. Submit yourselves therefore to God. Resist the devil, and he will flee from you. Draw nigh to God, and he will draw nigh to you....

JAMES 4:5–8

❧

It's also important to note that according to Scripture, envy can destroy our spirit as well as our health.

❧

A sound heart is the life of the flesh:
But envy the rottenness of the bones.

PROVERBS 14:30

❧

I'm ashamed to admit this, but on one occasion I actually played my "look at me" trump card with a rude medical receptionist. It all started rather innocently. I called to make a doctor's appointment for a prescription refill, and she began to lecture me for letting it expire in the first place. I tried to explain that my specialist had retired, that he had prescribed the medications, and that my multiple refills were finally up. I hadn't noticed, because normally, my doctor would just call in the refill if the pharmacy had any questions. Now I needed to go through my primary physician to take care of this situation.

For some reason (let's just call it the receptionist having a bad day), the gal decided to cop a snotty attitude that just wouldn't quit. I tried everything. I tried explaining myself again. I tried politeness: "You can catch more bees with honey." But finally, when her condescending attitude just wouldn't let up, I pulled out my official "I'm an author" trump card. "Look," I said to her firmly, "I'm a writer. I think I know enough to realize when I need to call the doctor."

Even as the words came tumbling out of my mouth, I thought to myself, Wow, I can't believe I'm stooping to this ridiculous level just to impress this gal. Oddly enough, though, it worked. She did stop her snide behavior, and she straightened herself out long enough to pass the information on to the physician. Problem solved. However, deep inside I wondered, What in the world did my being an author have to do with the necessity of a medical phone call? Absolutely nothing! It all boiled down to the following: I wanted her to respect me, so I pulled a cocky explanation out of my hat. Although it worked, I'm not proud of myself, and I'm happy to say that I've tried hard to avoid that pitfall again.

DON'T FEAR YOUR OWN SUCCESS

Aside from those who carry lofty dreams and pursue them with all their might, there are just as many good people who desperately fear their own success. They fight against themselves because they fear that if they are too successful, their lives will become chaotic and they will lose the security of what they know best.

I've met people (especially women) who've struggled with weight and then discovered they were staying heavy because they were actually afraid of looking good. They didn't want their friends, their mates, or even casual acquaintances to become so envious of them that their relationships might be damaged in the process.

How often have you known someone who was quite attractive before the wedding but afterward her partner sabotaged her looks because of basic jealousy? I've seen it happen. Insecurity and envy can do horrible things. By encouraging their partners to be overweight, some folks are convinced they can insure the success of their marriages. In their envious minds, their spouses' successes, including their healthy body image, could mean defeat for themselves.

If you're in a situation like that, address it immediately. Don't allow yourself to remain unhealthy, or simply feel unattractive, just to keep your mate from becoming envious of the natural attention your more-confident self is bound to attract. Never punish yourself for your obvious success, whether it's on a personal level, an academic one, or within the boundaries of your career. Be all you want to be, and expect your loved ones to rejoice with you and happily come along for the ride.

Scripture teaches that strife often stems from unfulfilled desires that have turned into envy. If we want fulfillment, we should ask God for it rather than growing jealous of another's blessings.

From whence come wars and fightings among you? come they not hence, even of your lusts that war in your members? Ye lust, and have not: ye kill, and desire to have, and cannot obtain: ye fight and war, yet ye have not, because ye ask not. Ye ask, and receive not, because ye ask amiss, that ye may consume it upon your lusts.

JAMES 4:1–3

Some folks fear their own financial success because they believe their friends and relatives will be struck by jealousy. And they continue to live a struggling life so that they don't rock the boat. Some fear successful career moves because they might make coworkers or loved ones envious and therefore change the very fiber of those relationships. So instead of flying for all it's worth, they reluctantly stay in jobs they don't like to insure that they won't make others uncomfortable.

We all want to be loved. We all want to get along, but at the same time, we must recognize that fulfilling our desires and goals is our rightful blessing. We must trust that our true friends, our mates, and those who really care will continue to love us anyway.

Instead of striving with our loved ones and growing envious of their blessings, we should, according to Scripture, ask for what we need and grow in our own blessings as well.

Ask, and it shall be given you; seek, and ye shall find; knock, and it shall be opened unto you: for every one that asketh receiveth; and he that seeketh findeth; and to him that knocketh it shall be opened. Or what man is there of you, whom if his son ask bread, will he give him a stone? Or if he ask a fish, will he give him a serpent? If ye then, being evil, know how to give good gifts unto your children, how much more

shall your Father which is in heaven give good things to them that ask
him? Therefore whatsoever ye would that men should do to you, do ye
even so to them: for this is the law and the prophets.

MATTHEW 7:7–12

✢

Scripture also shows us that we should support one another rather than getting caught up in petty jealousy. Together, through prayer, we can realize our dreams.

✢

Verily I say unto you, Whatsoever ye shall bind on earth shall be bound
in heaven: and whatsoever ye shall loose on earth shall be loosed in
heaven. Again I say unto you, That if two of you shall agree on earth as
touching any thing that they shall ask, it shall be done for them of my
Father which is in heaven. For where two or three are gathered together
in my name, there am I in the midst of them.

MATTHEW 18:18–20

✢

Fear of success, because of the impact it may have on relationships, is not entirely unfounded. I've experienced negative reactions to my own success time and time again. Some friends who had stood by me when I struggled and who had supported me in my dreams turned on a dime when they saw me receive my long-awaited blessings. Yes, when my dreams—whether they were financial, personal, or professional—began to come true, some people became distant. No, I was not flaunting my success (okay, maybe just to the rude medical receptionist), but through no fault of my own, the spirit of envy put a barrier between me and their previously open hearts.

A couple years ago, we bought a new home. A friend wanted to see it and made a lunch date to come over. While driving through our community, she grasped every opportunity possible to insult the place where I lived. The conversation was merciless: The houses were overpriced; the oak trees were doomed to die before their time, surely leaving our property values sinking into the holes they'd leave behind. You name it, she said it. When we went to lunch at the local country club, she manipulated her chair, sitting with her back to the view of the golf course, almost to spite the natural beauty that was clearly surrounding her. Did I see right through her behavior? You bet I did. She was obviously experiencing enormous bouts of envy and didn't know how to handle them except to try to bring me down with insults. Well, it didn't work. I still love my home and my neighborhood, and when I go to lunch, I'm not afraid to look out at the spectacular view as I embrace the oak trees, the wildlife, and the open space and thank God every minute for my blessings.

But jealous souls will not be answered so;
They are not ever jealous for the cause,
But jealous for they're jealous. It is a monster
Begot upon itself, born on itself.

WILLIAM SHAKESPEARE

In all fairness, I can't judge anyone's natural struggles with envy. Yes, I've been there myself. As an author, I've often helped other struggling writers, and I am ashamed to admit that a couple of times, once I saw them beginning to succeed, there was a part of me that watched to make sure they didn't surpass my level of success. Is that wrong? Of course it is. But, is it human nature? You betcha! So now that I'm aware of my own inclination toward envy, I prayerfully watch my reactions, guard my heart, and attempt to change my own spirit into one of true, loving support.

But if it be a sin to covet honour,
I am the most offending soul alive.

WILLIAM SHAKESPEARE

When Leann was offered an impressive promotion, her expectations immediately shot through the roof. However, within days, she began to doubt herself. What if she'd have trouble collaborating with her coworkers on new and challenging projects? What if there would be inner-office tension? What if her promotion would create jealousy within the company? Finally, one day, as she sat down for her quiet prayer time, she began to hear that still, small voice inside her heart—the one that over the years she'd come to know as the voice of God. In that moment, Leann realized that the real reason she didn't want the promotion was not because she feared failure, but because she feared success. Hmmmm. Talk about a reality check.

Once Leann discovered her true feelings, her doubts came pouring out. Would success change her friendships, her marriage, her very life as she knew it? Leann responded by prayerfully deciding to take the job challenge, knowing that her true and worthy relationships could withstand success, and the envy that might on occasion accompany it, as much as they could withstand the disappointment of failure.

So, although we are all aware that our success may invoke a bit of envy in even our closest loved ones, including our spouses, never let that be a reason to hold yourself back. Gently address the situation and bring your friends and your mate to a place of comfort where they can work through all of their personal insecurities. After all, you deserve to have loved ones who support your blessings instead of distancing themselves because of them.

❡ *Confess your envy.* First, admit it to yourself. Analyze what brings fear to your heart regarding your mate's success. Confess it to God, then finally to your spouse. Admission to yourself, God, and others is essential to working past your personal fears and coming to a place where you can truly rejoice in your partner's blessings.

❡ *Be supportive.* Instead of working against your mate's success, work toward it. Perhaps you can help out so he can fulfill his dream. Perhaps you simply need to offer an encouraging word when he's just about to give up.

❡ *Don't compete with your spouse.* Although competition can motivate our lives, don't allow it to take over your home. Support expresses joy over your loved one's blessings. Competition often reveals envy and a desire to overshadow each other. Allow both of your lights to shine like beacons. Rather than competing, rejoice in the special nature of your individual gifts.

¶ *Throw out the green-eyed monster.* Nip jealousy in the bud. Never tolerate a controlling, angry, distrustful relationship filled with suspicion. However, if your spouse has genuine discomfort about your behavior or relationships, be willing to talk it over reasonably. If need be, alter your behavior to bring a sense of comfort to him.

¶ *Don't feed envy.* It's fine to be proud of your accomplishments, but if insecurities lead you to flaunt yourself in front of others, including your spouse, be aware that you are dangerously fueling the fire of envy.

¶ *Don't fear your own success.* Don't allow the fear that others will become envious to keep you from your dreams. Your true friends, and a spouse who genuinely loves you, will support your goals, not seek to defeat your rising spirit. Be the best you can be, and expect your mate to rejoice with you as you reach new levels of blessing.

IV.

LOVE IS NOT PROUD

Humility—sometimes it can be a bitter pill to swallow. Yet when we approach life with a soft and tender spirit, our loved ones typically respond in kind, making our relationships smoother. To accomplish this, we must present an unassuming attitude to those around us without being afraid of losing who we are in the process. Humility, in its purest form, opens our spirit to God's eternal blessings.

In order to better our relationships, including our marriages, we must remain humble before our Creator, for God himself is drawn to the meek.

❧

For thus saith the high and lofty One
That inhabiteth eternity, whose name is Holy;
I dwell in the high and holy place,
With him also that is of a contrite and humble spirit,
To revive the spirit of the humble,
And to revive the heart of the contrite ones.

ISAIAH 57:15

❧

Jesus also spoke of coming to God with a humble, childlike heart. He is ready and willing to hear our cries, our needs, and our prayers.

❧

At the same time came the disciples unto Jesus, saying, Who is the great-
est in the kingdom of heaven? And Jesus called a little child unto him,
and set him in the midst of them. And said, Verily I say unto you,
Except ye be converted, and become as little children, ye shall not enter

into the kingdom of heaven. Whosoever shall humble himself as this little child, the same is greatest in the kingdom of heaven.

MATTHEW 18:1–4

❧

WHEN YOU'RE WRONG, SAY SO

Do you have a problem admitting when you're wrong? If so, join the crowd. Pride is part of our human nature. After all, everyone likes to be right. I know I do. However, the ability to own up to our mistakes, reveal our frailties, and acknowledge the fact that at any given moment we might just be wrong is essential to staying humble.

❧

Sometimes I wonder if men and women really suit each other. Perhaps they should live next door and just visit now and then.

KATHARINE HEPBURN

❧

As hard as it might be for you to admit, remember that there may actually be another side to the issues surrounding you. The mere acknowledgment that you are not the final authority is the beginning of humility. God honors this virtue, and people immediately respond favorably to its warmth. Others are instinctively drawn in by the tender aspects of modesty and are equally touched by its sincerity.

❧

Humility is a virtue all preach, none practise;
and yet everybody is content to hear.

JOHN SELDEN

❧

The opposite of meekness, of course, is pride. If you display an arrogant spirit, others will automatically move back. They'll have difficulty sharing their hearts, their thoughts, and their points of view for fear of having their feelings trampled upon by a somewhat dominant personality. They will become, either in a subtle fashion or quite obviously, standoffish, distant, and unsure of their desire to come closer.

In the last seventeen years, my husband has been wrong on only one occasion (or at least that's what he's clearly admitted to). However, I am grateful for his ability to reveal humility on what I consider to be a deeper level. It's true, if I bring up a topic that I feel requires his acknowledgment of wrongdoing, he often has trouble admitting his error outright or officially saying he's sorry. But what I prefer, and what does show sincere meekness, is that he genuinely takes to heart what I've said. How do I know this to be so? Immediately after our conversation, I will notice substantial behavioral changes from my husband that thankfully continue from that moment forward.

No, I'm not talking about anything dramatic here—just simple things. Perhaps I've gone to him and said, "You know, honey, when we walk through a store, you always rush off, and I feel literally left behind." I can almost guarantee that Patrick will say, "I don't think I've ever done that to you." Yet from that moment on, my husband will proceed to walk considerably slower, directly by my side. Is that a perfect show of humility? No. But in the case of many individuals, myself included, we're more likely to admit our mistakes and say we're sorry, but we don't necessarily change our behavior at all. Sure, I'd love for my husband to admit verbally when he's wrong, but I'd rather have sincere change than empty words any day. Patrick needs to work on the aspect of humility that requires him to confess his errors, while I need to concentrate on following up my easy-to-offer apologies with real, honest-to-goodness change.

Many years ago, when Kathy and Martin's daughter was going through the notorious terrible twos, she had trouble saying "I'm sorry." When she did something wrong and they asked her to apologize, she'd manipulate the word "sorry" to maintain an air of control and a personal sense of superiority. In place of "sorry," she'd offer up "sor" instead. For anyone

who might question this, no, she did not have difficulty speaking. Her verbal skills, her parents insist, were more than adequate. What the situation
boiled down to was that their little girl wanted to maintain a sense of pride
by simply pretending to apologize.

At first, being typical in-a-hurry parents, Kathy and Martin fell for it
completely, thinking she'd done what was asked. Yet as they began to listen
more closely, they realized she was only falsifying humility by sort of
apologizing, but not really. How interesting that even a 2-year-old would
have the instinct to refuse to admit when she was wrong, seeing her sole
purpose to fight the basic aspect of being humble. Is it any wonder that
even as adults we're often caught up in the same struggles?

A few years ago, my son, Nicholas, had similar early-age concerns. When
confronted with a mistake, instead of admitting wrongdoing and fixing the
problem, he'd look at us as if we were nuts, refusing to acknowledge he'd
ever done a thing. I remember one particular afternoon when he had tossed
a ball onto the roof. First, let me say that it wasn't a big deal. Quite frankly,
nobody cared. However, because we knew he was struggling with humble
accountability, my husband decided to put Nick to the test. He quietly
asked our son how the ball got onto the roof. "I don't know," Nick insisted.
I didn't do it." I asked Patrick if maybe someone else could have thrown it up
there. "No," my husband explained, "I watched him do it, and I just want to
see how long it will take him to admit the truth, apologize, and move on."

Well, let me tell you, it was a long wait. An entire afternoon later, Nick finally fessed up. Was the whole escapade a giant crime? No. But was his refusal to take responsibility in a humble and honest way a problem? Yes it was!

Taking time to teach our children the importance of humility and of being accountable toward others was a vital part of our parenting. I'm happy to say, our kids have successfully worked through it. In fact, my son now confesses things to us we don't even want to know about. On occasion, Nick comes home from school with stories like this one: "Mom, today on the bus, I bumped into someone." I giggle, because at the age of 10, he's come full circle and doesn't quite know where to draw the line between when it's necessary to humbly admit a mistake and when it simply isn't worth mentioning. However, I'll take that until he learns the proper balance, so I don't have to worry about him hiding his mistakes, lying, and refusing to acknowledge any wrongdoing at all.

If you were not taught humility when you were growing up, don't give up now. It's never too late to strengthen that virtue. If you can't admit mistakes or worse yet, you refuse to change your behavior, make a sincere attempt to approach your loved ones with humility. If nothing else, consider meekness as a way to smooth the path before you, make your spouse feel more at ease, and allow more open communication to come your way.

LET OTHERS HAVE THE LAST WORD

On occasion, I visit a political Website filled with up-to-the-minute news, events, and sometimes mildly hot topics. The banter can get rather feisty, with strong, articulate opinions flying back and forth. Although most debates are handled in good taste, once in a while, they become a nuclear explosion of intense e-mails. About a year ago, I got so wrapped up in a few controversial discussions that I practically submitted a letter daily. And I wasn't the only one. I found myself checking the site numerous times an hour, in a rather strange, obsessive fashion. When I discovered posters who disagreed with me, I'd be compelled to write in immediately to "set them straight." Finally, one afternoon, realizing I was bordering on a serious addiction, I said to my husband, "You know, I think I have a problem. I've discovered I'm compelled to have the last word, and more importantly, I feel an overpowering need to be right." My husband, bless his heart, smiled and quietly said, "Candy, are you telling me you just realized that about yourself?" Yes, sometimes the sick are the last ones to know.

Understanding that I and a few of my online pals were just inches away from needing a twelve-step program to deliver us from our addiction, I knew it was time to get a prayerful grip. For me, confessing my weakness before God, signing on to that Web site less, letting others respectfully have their say without my being compelled to reply every time, and realizing that I didn't actually need to have the last word or be right were steps toward my breakthrough to personal freedom (not to mention, no doubt, a huge relief to the other online contributors).

How many of us feel compelled to have the last word within our marriages? Do you need to be right all the time—even if it takes you all night to convince your husband of your side? Tell me, what have you genuinely accomplished in the end if you've made him feel distant and uncomfortable? Try to remember that gracious humility works wonders with our neighbors, our world, and yes, even our marriages.

DON'T RUB IT IN

To encourage meekness, allow your spouse to retain some form of dignity even within the framework of his mistakes. Whatever you do, don't rub them in. This will only make it harder for your husband to admit his errors next time.

Years ago, Marlene's husband, Jack, came home from work to say he'd received a speeding ticket. Instead of kindly offering words of encouragement, she replied, "Well, good. You drive too fast anyway. Maybe now you'll slow down." What happened after that? They experienced an entire two days of silence. He was mad, and she was mad at him for being mad.

Eventually, of course, they worked it out. In fact, a couple days later, Jack gave Marlene a card that included a sweet note inside. In it, he admitted that he shouldn't have been speeding and that he shouldn't have offered her the silent treatment; however, that was only after he had written, "but you shouldn't have rubbed it in either." And he was right. Marlene immediately confessed her wrongdoing as well and began to exhibit her own sense of humility.

SET AN EXAMPLE

Recently my husband took my son grocery shopping on an extremely blustery winter day. After they parked in the crowded lot, he carefully opened the door to make his exit. Unfortunately, the wind caught the metal frame and flung it open faster than Patrick had intended. What happened? A big, fat ding in the car door next to his. Now, let me make this clear—no one appeared to be watching. Only my son and my husband truly knew what had happened. So did Patrick drive away, pretend it didn't occur, blame it on an act of God because of nasty weather? No. He humbled himself, swallowed the fact that he'd be doomed to pay a hefty insurance deductible, and left a note for the other driver with an apology, our accountability information, and our home phone number.

Later that evening, the gentleman of the other car telephoned. He and my husband chatted for a minute while the surprised man kept repeating how flabbergasted he was that Patrick left a note in the first place. "I hope I'd do the same thing in a similar situation," he said. My husband replied, "Of course you would. We all have to take responsibility in this world for our actions."

So, you may wonder, are we doomed to get a whoppin' insurance bill? Of course. Will it be pleasant? No, I'm sure it will not. However, the example my husband set for our son and for the other gentleman, as well as the fact that Patrick can retain his peaceful conscience, will be worth every last dime. After all, if nothing else, we should always remember that God is watching. Ultimately, he is our audience.

DON'T BE AFRAID TO SERVE OTHERS

Before anyone gets excited, let me just say that service is a two-way street. When we love one another, service is not a duty or a chore—it's a joy. Whether a mother nurtures and comforts her sick child, a father changes his infant's diaper, a wife does something that makes her husband smile, or a husband returns the favor in kind, it's not work, not slavery, not a chore, but rather an automatic expression of love.

That said, we all need time for ourselves, and many of us get so busy serving others that we forget to indulge in our own much-needed rest and comfort. Without a doubt, each of us craves time for personal hobbies and joyful moments—catching an old movie, reading a great book, taking a hot bubble bath, going on a long walk, shopping, or having lunch with friends. Yet when our cup is full, we need to realize that our place in the world is not "Me first" and need to humble ourselves and make our loved ones' lives a little better just for our being there.

As you're probably aware, many people vie for leadership roles within the religious world. Ministry positions seem important, and for many individuals who don't grasp the true humble calling, these positions can represent great personal accomplishment and status.

When John wanted to offer humble service, he took it upon himself to sweep the entry of the sanctuary, clean the bathrooms, and empty the trash. Were those spiritually glamorous jobs? Of course not. Was he leading Bible studies, teaching Sunday school, or holding any prominent position of authority? No. However, in humility, he chose to serve God quietly behind the scenes and strictly out of sincere and devoted love. Eventually, when John's gentle spirit was noticed, he was offered a teaching job in the church. Why? God saw his simple status and promoted him to higher service. Genuine humility is often honored, while grandstanding rarely brings eternal blessings.

So, instead of forcing our strength, our pride, or our presence on others, including our spouses, Scripture teaches us to remain humble and not think too highly of ourselves, for God alone will lift us up:

And he put forth a parable to those which were bidden, when he marked how they chose out the chief rooms; saying unto them, When thou art bidden of any man to a wedding, sit not down in the highest room; lest a more honourable man than thou be bidden of him; and he

that bade thee and him come and say to thee, Give this man place; and
thou begin with shame to take the lowest room. But when thou art
bidden, go and sit down in the lowest room; that when he that bade
thee cometh, he may say unto thee, Friend, go up higher: then shalt thou
have worship in the presence of them that sit at meat with thee. For
whosoever exalteth himself shall be abased; and he that humbleth
himself shall be exalted.

LUKE 14:7–11

༺

Once again, your humility is the genuine sign of God's own.

༺

Humble yourselves in the sight of the Lord, and he shall lift you up.

JAMES 4:10

༺

Remember, according to the deeper teachings of Scripture, we must
remain humble with each other. Then, in time, God himself will lift us up
to a place of honor.

…Yea, all of you be subject one to another, and be clothed with humility: for God resisteth the proud, and giveth grace to the humble. Humble yourselves therefore under the mighty hand of God, that he may exalt you in due time: casting all your care upon him; for he careth for you.

I PETER 5:5–7

Within your marriage, reaching out through humility might be as simple as offering your spouse a neck massage (I can promise you that my husband will laugh when he reads this, because I'm a bit lazy in this department), baking his favorite treat, or encouraging him to take time for himself, even if only for a short, but much appreciated, afternoon.

Humility, that low, sweet root
From which all heavenly virtues shoot.

THOMAS MOORE

BE EQUAL, BUT CONTINUE TO SERVE

I almost hesitate to include this section, because some people might say, "Yikes, by now don't we all know we're equal?" Unfortunately, I'm not so sure we all do. Believe it or not, I still run across folks who are convinced that serving another shows a sign of inferiority and is mandatory by only one spouse (yes, usually the wife). Thankfully, most of us understand that that's just not the way our Creator intended us to live.

Of course we are each important. We are each valuable. But to put another ahead of ourselves, even if only for a moment, shows great humility and grace, which will, in time, be honored.

❧

For, brethren, ye have been called unto liberty; only use not liberty for an occasion to the flesh, but by love serve one another. For all the law is fulfilled in one word, even in this; Thou shalt love thy neighbour as thyself.

GALATIANS 5:13-14

❧

When you love your spouse and hold him in a special place of blessing, this is not a heavy cloak of subservience, but one of equality and joy. For when you give, you are sure to receive.

Be humble, make your mate number one, and expect to be treated the same. Being humble does not mean becoming a doormat—far from it. In fact, the mere thought makes me shudder. Having humility means respecting yourself enough to expect the same treatment from others and offering service to those around you without fear of losing yourself in the process.

STAY HUMBLE BEFORE GOD

Without a spiritual side to marriage, much is left out of its original design and purpose. By remaining humble before God, by simply acknowledging that his reality, his presence, and his purpose are extremely important in our lives, we open ourselves up to a better understanding of our divine, eternal destiny.

Besides exhibiting humility toward our loved ones, reveal it to God in prayer. Joyfully, with praise, acknowledge who he is and the prominence he plays in your life, your relationships, and your marriage.

Make a joyful noise unto the LORD, all ye lands.
Serve the Lord with gladness:
Come before his presence with singing.
Know ye that the LORD he is God:
It is he that hath made us, and not we ourselves;

We are his people, and the sheep of his pasture.
Enter into his gates with thanksgiving,
And into his courts with praise:
Be thankful unto him, and bless his name.
For the LORD is good; his mercy is everlasting;
And his truth endureth to all generations.

PSALM 100

❧

How many people recite wedding vows and then proceed to throw God out of the marriage the minute they leave the altar? In many cases, God's hardly invited to the reception. Then we wonder why we're often in trouble.

By acknowledging that we can't make it on our own and that God is our higher power, the one with the wisdom to know the road we should travel, we show humility that will overflow into our marriages and all aspects of our world.

Do you know anyone who is an absolute control freak? Are you one? In a sense, the desire to maintain that sort of ultimate control is a form of pride. Whether they're in the workplace, in their homes, or at a social club, controlling individuals have to do it all. Yes, they are exhausted. Yes, they are running themselves into the ground, but in their own minds, they are convinced no one can do it like they can.

❦

None shall rule but the humble,
And none but Toil shall have.

RALPH WALDO EMERSON

❦

Perhaps we're sure we are right. Perhaps we think we know better than everyone, but when we genuinely listen to one another and, even more importantly, bring our concerns to God, we show great humility and great wisdom.

❦

…The foolishness of God is wiser than men; and the weakness of God is stronger than men. For ye see your calling, brethren, how that not many wise men after the flesh, not many mighty, not many noble, are called: but God hath chosen the foolish things of the world to confound the wise; and God hath chosen the weak things of the world to confound the things which are mighty; and base things of the world, and things which are despised, hath God chosen, yea, and things, which are not, to bring to nought things that are: that no flesh should glory in his presence.

I CORINTHIANS 1:25–29

❦

I know a gentleman who no matter what job he takes convinces himself within days that no one can run the company like he can. So year after year, he continues to complain that wherever he goes and whatever he does, no one else can do it like him. Is it any wonder, he explains, that he's exhausted, stressed, and absolutely overwhelmed? But what do you think are the odds that he always winds up working with losers? While others have no problem finding folks to delegate responsibilities to, how is it that he always ends up in a department filled with flakes? The reality is, it has nothing to do with others at all, and everything to do with himself. This man clearly needs to control it all because he's filled with an enormous sense of pride. In order to break free from this exhausting approach, he must come to terms with the fact that others may be able to offer positive contributions as well. He must come to the realization that he's not the be-all and end-all of employees.

How often do we take that same pride-filled attitude into our lives when we fear turning things over to God? By admitting we can't do it all, whether it's handling our finances, our jobs, or our marriages, we are displaying a humble spirit that finally allows God to play a part in our lives. We must tenderly let go in order to allow God to take his rightful place beside us. After all, he's a gentleman. He won't force his way in. God has to be invited by a humble host.

So, don't forget to include God in your relationships. Prayer is an act of humility. Think about it. By reaching out to heaven, we are admitting we're not center of the universe. We're admitting we don't have all the answers. And more importantly, we're acknowledging that someone else does.

Praying for our marriage and for all of our relationships demonstrates a truly humble spirit that will be richly rewarded with spiritual, as well as practical, results.

TIPS TO TAKE AWAY

¶ *When you're wrong, say so.* Then go one step further. Begin to make real behavioral changes. Words can be cheap. Be sure to act on your acknowledgments.

¶ *Don't rub it in.* Allow your spouse and others around you to feel a sense of dignity as they show humility in your presence. Never rub it in or make them feel low for displaying meekness. Instead, encourage them by doing what God does: Lift them up to a place of appreciative honor for exhibiting this wonderful virtue.

¶ *Set an example.* By living a life of genuine humility—admitting when you're wrong and taking responsibility for your own actions—you set a wonderful example for your spouse, your children, and the world around you. Goodness is catchy. Pass it on.

¶ *Don't be afraid to serve others.* And that includes your husband. Humble service is not a sign of weakness, but of strength. Offer him (and others) innumerable simple blessings. Surely, your good deeds will be abundantly returned.

¶ *Be equal, but continue to serve.* Remember, giving is the essence of love. We must remain humble to display a heart of generosity. Humility and service do not make you inferior. In actuality, they reveal that you clearly understand your greatest eternal value.

¶ *Stay humble before God.* Reserve a special prayer time each day. Bring your needs, your loved one's needs, and yes, your marriage before God. Don't be too proud to ask for help. Then, stand back and watch your life begin to change for the better.

V.

Love Is Not
Easily Provoked

No, love is not easily provoked. It does not lend itself to angry or hostile demands. Love, in actuality, strives to display an overwhelming abundance of gentleness and understanding.

❧

Anger kills both laughter and joy;
What greater foe is there than anger?

TIRUVALLUVAR

KEEP THE PEACE

Have you ever been in a room full of noisy, rather wild, out-of-control children? Although overall we tend to appreciate their lively, youthful mannerisms and joyful spirits, we are more likely to be annoyed by the distraction of other people's kids than we are by our own. Love, the commitment we have to those we're bonded to, allows us to have the patience necessary to understand behavior through the sacred eyes of grace.

Similarly, when we commit ourselves to our mates, when the marriage vows are taken, we should embrace a level of understanding that dispels the initial reaction to become easily provoked without ample cause. Let's face it—no one enjoys being caught up in the turmoil of another's frustration. Although arguments are sure to develop, let them be addressed with the peaceful intention of bringing unity to your home. Yes, clear the air. Yes, address your concerns, but never allow hostility or angry words to overwhelm the oneness of your relationship.

❧

My advice to you is to get married. If you find a good wife, you'll be happy; if not, you'll become a philosopher.

SOCRATES

❧

Of course, serious disputes can erupt during legitimate discussions, but on occasion, they emerge from trivial matters that become unnecessarily important.

For example, one afternoon several years ago, I asked my husband what he thought of my new haircut. Well, I had asked a straight question, but evidently, I wasn't looking for a straight answer. When Patrick told me he preferred my hair the way it had been before my somewhat overdone clip, I became obviously annoyed. Immediately after rolling my eyes, I fired off a slew of follow-up questions: Would he prefer me as a blond or as a brunet? Did he prefer my hair short, as it was then, or medium, as it had been before?

Patrick was not willing to fall for my ridiculous game twice, so he tried to hedge his bets by telling me that ultimately the entire choice was up to me. As long as I liked it, he insisted, that was all that really mattered.

Even though I gave him credit for his finely tuned diplomatic strategy, I wasn't going to let him off the hook with such an easy escape, so I kept on. Finally, after he felt questioned to death, my daughter entered the room. She'd been watching a kids' show and found the proposed plot hysterical. "Hey, Dad," she asked, "would you be willing to earn a million dollars if it meant you had to have the head of a fish for a month?" As I began to giggle at such a ridiculous question, my husband leaned over to me and said, "I don't know. Hey, Candy, what's the right answer?"

Yikes, I thought, what in the world have I created? Here was a man who meant well but now understood that no matter what he said, he was going to be in the doghouse. Taking the odd question my daughter had brought to our attention as a sign from God that I was being every bit as ridiculous, I immediately apologized to my husband. By the way, since that time, I do as Patrick suggested. If I like my hair, outfit, or perfume, I don't ask his opinion unless, of course, I'm willing to receive an answer that might not suit my desires.

So, always allow your disagreements to be constructive discussions of viewpoints rather than vicious attacks on each other. Address the behavior in question, not the individual. By doing so, you will keep the door wide open for change without making your spouse feel you're on the rampage, therefore causing him to become defensive and ultimately allowing hostility to triumph.

Through prayer, Scripture reveals, we can gain a sense of peace that will overflow onto others:

❧

Peace I leave with you, my peace I give unto you: not as the world giveth, give I unto you. Let not your heart be troubled, neither let it be afraid.

JOHN 14:27

❧

Yes, life can be chaotic, and peace is a virtue not easily attained. Yet with prayer, Scripture teaches, God can fill our hearts with a sense of peace despite our surroundings:

✦

These things I have spoken unto you, that in me ye might have peace. In the world ye shall have tribulation: but be of good cheer; I have overcome the world.

JOHN 16:33

✦

WORK THROUGH PROBLEMS

Hot buttons—we all have them. We all live with certain issues or behaviors that set us on edge. To put this in perspective, think about your genuine concerns. In fact, it's probably a good idea to write them down. Then go over every part of your list in great detail. Which items are deal breakers? Which are simply preferences, and which need to be addressed and changed before you can continue on in a healthy relationship?

Next, go to your spouse in a calm and loving spirit and address your priorities. If your life is filled with constant interruptions and you do not conceive of ever having an opportune moment to work things through quietly, arrange for a special time and location where you can have your heart-to-heart with minimal distractions. But first, choose the location wisely. Hashing it out in the center of a busy café or while stuck in an enormous traffic jam or even when the phone is ringing off the hook is probably not the ideal situation.

Then, calmly share your thoughts. You may find that your concerns are understood, respected, and acted on immediately. Or you may be greeted with a blank stare or, worse yet, denial that your claims are valid at all. Whatever the reaction, continue with a calm spirit. If you are sure of the importance of your issues and you've decided it's vital that change occur, calmly but firmly make that clear. Although yelling can be tempting, such displays of over-the-top anger will not solve your problems, but will likely intensify the distance between you and your spouse.

Now ask yourself, Are there any hot buttons I can learn to ignore? Remember, your spouse surely has a mental list of things you need to work on as well. So ask yourself, Am I also open to change? Addressing issues openly works both ways, and change must come from both spouses to be successful.

Each of us sees life through our own individual perspective, and for many folks, the world tends to revolve around them in all its glory. When Michele was shopping for a new outfit at the mall, her husband, Jim, casually mentioned to the saleswoman, "My wife used to dress up, but now, I never see her in anything but sweatsuits." The saleswoman, not missing a beat and obviously not the least bit concerned about her commission, leaned over, patted Jim's belly, and said, "And I bet you didn't have this before you got married either." Touché. She'd hit the nail right on the head, and Jim knew he'd been one-upped. So he smiled sheepishly and admitted she was right. Now, that doesn't mean he still wouldn't prefer to see Michele dressed up more often, but he realized in that moment that no one is perfect, not even himself. Ah, he who lives in a glass house…

Scripture admonishes us to accept others with a spirit of love:

Judge not, that ye be not judged. For with what judgment ye judge, ye shall be judged: and with what measure ye mete, it shall be measured to you again. And why beholdest thou the mote that is in thy brother's eye, but considerest not the beam that is in thine own eye? Or who wilt thou say to thy brother, Let me pull out the mote out of thine eye; and behold, a beam is in thine own eye? Thou hypocrite, first cast out the beam out of thine own eye; and then shalt thou see clearly to cast out the mote out of thy brother's eye.

MATTHEW 7:1–5

DON'T THRIVE ON DRAMA

Do you know people like that? Or worse yet, are you an individual who feeds off a chaotic environment and who gets bored, or even unnerved, by a peaceful existence? Do you create chaos because, oddly enough, that's what's most comfortable for you? If so, examine your reactions to life's calmest situations, and ask God for the desire to live in peace. Although it may not appear natural to you, serenity is not boring. It's a blessing.

When I was 17, my older sister, Spring, died of cancer. It was a tragic loss, and our family never truly recovered from it. It's taken great prayer and many years to overcome my intense feelings of negativity. I always presumed that when life looked its happiest, something terrible was sure to happen. My friend Lisa can attest to the fact that early in my marriage, I was convinced I was dying just about every other week. The reality is, I was perfectly healthy, but because such a horrible reality had happened to my sister, it made me feel that either I or another of my loved ones would also be taken at a young age. It took years for me to accept that good things also happen to people and that I should anticipate the positive instead of always expecting the worst.

I've known folks who grew up in a hostile environment and who once they were married sought to create tension within their own households. Strangely enough, as much as they craved a peaceful existence, chaos was the only life they knew. If that's your M.O., bring your mind-set and your preconditioning toward a nonproductive and ever dramatic life to God. Ask for the desire and the ability to maintain a peaceful marriage. After all, peace is God's gift to you. Relax and enjoy it.

❧

Forgo your anger for a moment,
and save yourself a hundred days of trouble.

CHINESE PROVERB

❧

Scripture teaches us God's response to angry, dramatic overtures. We can learn a lesson from his mercy and grace.

❧

The LORD is merciful and gracious,
Slow to anger, and plenteous in mercy.
He will not always chide:
Neither will he keep his anger for ever.
He hath not dealt with us after our sins;
Nor rewarded us according to our iniquities.
For as the heaven is high above the earth,
So great is his mercy toward them that fear him.

As far as the east is from the west,
So far hath he removed our transgressions from us.

PSALM 103:8-12

※

Even Jesus taught his followers that an angry spirit is unacceptable to God. He expressed in detail how we could make peace with God, with ourselves, and with each other:

※

For I say unto you, That except your righteousness shall exceed the right-
eousness of the scribes and Pharisees, ye shall in no case enter into the
kingdom of heaven.

Ye have heard that it was said by them of old time, Thou shalt not
kill; and whosoever shall kill shall be in danger of the judgment: but I
say unto you, That whosoever is angry with his brother without a cause
shall be in danger of the judgment: and whosoever shall say to his broth-
er, Raca, shall be in danger of the council: but whosoever shall say, Thou
fool, shall be in danger of hell fire. Therefore if thou bring thy gift to the
altar, and there rememberest that thy brother hath ought against thee;
leave there thy gift before the altar, and go thy way; first be reconciled to

thy brother, and then come and offer thy gift. Agree with thine adver-
sary quickly....

❧

As a couple, you should always seek God's higher purpose. Discover, through prayer and growth, that God loves you both immensely. Believe that he has great and wonderful things in store for your life and that hostility is not a part of his awesome plan.

KEEP IT POSITIVE

We all respond to positive strokes and feedback. So, keeping that in mind, rather than coming to your husband with a list of only his flaws, be sure to offer positive input as well. Tell your loved one what he is doing right. Show him how much you appreciate his better qualities. Once you've done that, then explain what areas you feel need improvement. In this way, your spouse will be less defensive and will understand that you're sharing your concerns not out of cruelty but with a heart that's founded in love.

The wisdom of Scripture encourages us to never allow anger or bitterness to grasp our lives and our relationships:

❧

Follow peace with all men, and holiness, without which no man shall
see the Lord: looking diligently lest any man fail of the grace of God;
lest any root of bitterness springing up trouble you, and thereby many
be defiled.

HEBREWS 12:14–15

❧

However, be sure to be genuine with this approach. Barbara's friend loves to use this positive-with-the-negative tactic. Yet Barbara has absolutely no trouble seeing right through this gal's hidden agenda. For example, recently she called to say, "Barbara, you looked marvelous the other night at the party. Your outfit was adorable. And don't worry, I'm sure nobody noticed your panty lines except me. But really, Barbara, you looked stunning."

Ouch! Gee, thanks! Her friend has tried this approach so often that Barbara's begun to duck and cover whenever the friend offers a backhanded compliment, because she knows an insult is sure to come her way.

Ancient custom had those with a repentant heart visibly display their sincerity by placing ashes upon their heads. Scripture teaches us that we're more likely to encourage others toward true change, or repentance, if we're gracious with them rather than forceful:

If thine enemy be hungry, give him bread to eat;
And if he be thirsty, give him water to drink:
For thou shalt heap coals of fire upon his head,
And the LORD shall reward thee.
The north wind driveth away rain:
So doth an angry countenance a backbiting tongue.

PROVERBS 25:21-23

A few years ago, Heather's son, Kyle, had a teacher who called her with a long list of complaints. (By the way, this is the only teacher who ever expressed such negativity in Kyle's life.) She said Kyle was doing horribly in math and seemed blankly distracted in class. After an extensive complaint list, she ended the conversation with, "He really is a darling boy. I'm so glad I have him in my class." Uh-huh, sure. Heather was really going to fall for that. Incidentally, when all was said and done, Kyle's grades were wonderful, and his test scores were at the top of the state percentile. Go figure.

Keeping this in mind, there is a way to approach your mate with a list of his positive attributes (but do it with sincerity) and then with areas you feel still need improvement. For example: "Honey, I love the fact you always call when you're bringing someone home from work. It's considerate of you, and I do appreciate it. However, in the future, would you give me a little more notice so I can better prepare?" This example comes to mind easily because just this week, my husband didn't give me proper notice. He called to let me know his friend was coming home with him, but unfortunately, he notified me from the front entrance of our gated community, giving me less than two minutes of warning. Intentions? Good. Planning? Not so good.

If you're dealing with a workaholic, someone who rarely checks into his real life at home, you can offer your observations and desire for change on a positive note. For example, instead of getting angry and offering words like, "You are never home. I'm tired of eating dinner by myself!" How about trying something else? For example: "I realize you care about providing for our family, and I must say, you do a wonderful job. However, what I really want from you is time rather than money. I know your intentions are good, and I do appreciate that, but the result of your long hours is harming the most precious part of our relationship—being together."

Scripture teaches us much about loving, having a gracious and gentle spirit, and avoiding levels of anger that are ultimately destructive:

Be ye angry, and sin not: let not the sun go down upon your wrath: neither give place to the devil....Let no corrupt communication proceed out

of your mouth, but that which is good to the use of edifying, that it may
minister grace unto the hearers. And grieve not the holy Spirit of God,
whereby ye are sealed unto the day of redemption. Let all bitterness, and
wrath, and anger, and clamour, and evil speaking, be put away from
you, with all malice: and be ye kind one to another, tenderhearted,
forgiving one another, even as God for Christ's sake hath forgiven you.

EPHESIANS 4:26–32

❧

Always encourage your spouse with genuine, positive strokes. Then let him or her know your desire for change in areas that still need improvement. After all, you're more likely to see improvement when you approach issues with love and kindness instead of intense negativity.

GET HELP IF NEEDED

If you're in a relationship where explosive anger is present (whether it's verbal or physical), get help immediately. No one deserves to be the victim of another's out-of-control hostility. No one should be compelled to live in fear. You are not the cause of, nor are you responsible for fixing, another individual's outrage.

Scripture warns us about avoiding hostile people:

꒯

Make no friendship with an angry man;
And with a furious man thou shalt not go:
Lest thou learn his ways,
And get a snare to thy soul.

PROVERBS 22:24–25

꒯

If you're in an abusive situation, go to the police, a counselor, a member of your clergy, a family member, or a friend, but seek help immediately. Never be caught up in a false sense of shame or the belief that you are to blame for another's unacceptable behavior.

Once you're given help and advice, begin to act on it. Nancy had a friend who called daily to talk about her abusive husband. Nancy tried everything possible to help her bewildered caller. She offered her a place to stay. She gave her the number for safe houses and counselors. However, each time this woman hung up the phone, she proceeded to invite her husband back into their home. Then, believe it or not, the very next afternoon, the phone calls would start all over again.

Finally, after months of being caught up in this vicious cycle, Nancy realized that her friend, at that point in her life, had no intention of truly changing her circumstances. In reality, she had been given every opportunity to receive help, but she just wasn't ready for change.

I'm not suggesting we should ever forget those in need. What I'm saying is that the recipients must truly be ready for genuine help. If you're being abused, take help seriously. You may not get another chance to save your life.

TAKE YOUR ANGER TO GOD

We all have our weaknesses—downright flaws that are hard to control. For some of us, anger is one of them. If your days are filled with thoughts of life's unfairness toward you and of hostility toward others, take those feelings to God. Ask him to show you where you may need more understanding, more serenity, and a less judgmental spirit.

❧

Anger is a brief lunacy.

HORACE

❧

Through reflective moments, prayer time, and quiet meditations, you can be filled with a calmer, more peaceful spirit that lends itself to better relationships and is less likely to flare up unnecessarily.

Jesus taught us to find a quiet place to be alone and graciously seek God in prayer:

※

Take heed that ye do not your alms before men, to be seen of them: otherwise ye have no reward of your Father which is in heaven. Therefore when thou doest thine alms, do not sound a trumpet before thee, as the hypocrites do in the synagogues and in the streets, that they may have glory of men. Verily I say unto you, They have their reward. But when thou doest alms, let not thy left hand know what thy right hand doeth: that thine alms may be in secret: and thy Father which seeth in secret himself shall reward thee openly.

And when thou prayest, thou shall not be as the hypocrites are: for they pray standing in the synagogues and in the corners of the streets, that they may be seen of men. Verily I say unto you, They have their reward. But thou, when thou prayest, enter into thy closet, and when thou hast shut thy door, pray to thy Father which is in secret; and thy Father which seeth in secret shall reward thee openly. But when ye pray, use not vain repetitions, as the heathen do: for they think that they shall be heard for their much speaking. Be not ye therefore like unto them: for your Father knoweth what things ye have need of, before ye ask him. After this manner therefore pray ye:

Our Father which art in heaven, Hallowed be thy name. Thy king-
dom come, Thy will be done in earth, as it is in heaven. Give us this
day our daily bread. And forgive us our debts, as we forgive our debtors.
And lead us not into temptation, but deliver us from evil: For thine is
the kingdom, and the power, and the glory, for ever. Amen.

MATTHEW 6:1–13

Sometimes all it takes to bring us back to a proper, caring, noncon-
frontational perspective in the heat of a senseless argument is the odd
reactions we get from others. When my husband and I were on the last day
of our honeymoon (yes, petty arguments can begin even that early in the
long journey of marriage), he accidentally locked the keys in our rental car.
And, I want you to know, the vehicle was still running. So, after we both
shrugged our shoulders in disbelief, we managed to borrow a coat hanger
from a nearby driver in the parking lot. Then we meticulously jiggled it
around in the lock until we eventually got the door open, turned off the
engine, and retrieved our missing keys. Once our problem was solved, we
laughed about it for a moment and then went on our way, browsing through
adorable local shops and later indulging in a scrumptious seafood lunch.

Later that day on our way home, we decided to stop at my grandparents'
house for a short visit. Attempting to locate their home from another locale,

I gave Patrick the best directions I knew—directions, by the way, which weren't exactly correct. After getting lost several times and taking a few extensive, unintentional tours of the area, we finally made it to our destination.

As we got out of the car and walked up my grandparents' sidewalk, the tension of the long, lost drive finally overcame us. So when Patrick made a snide remark about my terrible navigating abilities, I immediately shot back with, "Well, at least I'm smart enough not to lock the car keys in a running vehicle!"

As we continued to snarl at each other, my grandmother opened the front door, giggling hysterically over two ridiculously grumpy newlyweds. Apparently, she'd heard us all the way from the curb and was obviously wondering how we'd ever make it past our first anniversary.

Patrick and I took one look at my grandmother's face and quickly apologized. In the purest way, her reaction gave us a wonderful attitude check and immediately put things back into perspective. Yes, it's never wise to make mountains out of molehills.

¶ *Keep the peace.* Make a conscious decision to bring peace to your spouse's life, to your marriage, and to your home. Refuse to spend time in senseless disputes, angry outbursts, or tense interactions. Instead, offer up a heart of goodwill toward your mate, expecting it to come full circle back to you.

¶ *Work through problems.* First, discover your own hot buttons. Then, address each of them calmly in a quiet, neutral, and private place. If at all possible, avoid hashing them out in a distracting or chaotic environment. Arguing in front of your mother-in-law at Thanksgiving is definitely not your best bet. Instead, go to a special place to deal with these issues in a calm and respectful tone.

¶ *Don't thrive on drama.* While intense relationships may seem exciting or even comfortable to you, seek God's best intentions for your marriage through a prayerful spirit. Then, begin to approach your relationship with the goal of achieving a peaceful, joyful existence rather than one based on intensity through negative interaction.

¶ *Keep it positive.* Although disagreements are bound to occur, try to keep your feelings in perspective. When approaching your husband, attempt to bring up his positive attributes while you also discuss the list of his less-than-desirable behaviors. In so doing, you'll keep your own thoughts in perspective, you'll continue to appreciate your loved one's good points, and you'll ultimately help your spouse accept what you say in the spirit in which it was intended instead of putting him immediately on the defense.

§   *Get help if needed.* Know that physical or emotional abuse is not acceptable—no matter what. Regardless of what anyone might express otherwise, you absolutely do not deserve it. Be aware of a safe place you can go where a nonjudgmental, loving ear awaits you.

§   *Take your anger to God.* Plan a special time and place when and where you can pray each day. Remember, it's impossible to instill a sense of peace in others when your own soul is filled with chaos. Through prayer, quiet reflective moments, and sacred meditations, God can fill your heart with calmness that's bound to overflow into a successful, loving marriage.

VI.

LOVE TRUSTS AND HOPES

Love believes all things and hopes all things. True love is based on faith. In order to extend ourselves better in gracious relationships, we must be open to faith, to trust, to believing the best in one another. Without those basic attributes, our relationships may be based on attraction but not necessarily on love.

❧

Hope elevates, and joy
Brightens his crest.

JOHN MILTON

ACCENTUATE THE POSITIVE

How often do we reap what we sow? This basic spiritual principle can work for or against us. If you sow corn, you shouldn't expect to reap a crop of tomatoes. If you sow nothing, you should understand you'll reap nothing in return (except maybe weeds). Yet in relationships, many folks sow negativity and still expect to reap positive results. Tell me, in what universe is that possible? That's just not how God set things in motion.

Scripture reveals the absolute importance of planting good "crops" in our lives, for ultimately we all reap what we sow:

❦

But this I say, He which soweth sparingly shall reap also sparingly; and he which soweth bountifully shall reap also bountifully. Every man according as he purposeth in his heart, so let him give; not grudgingly, or of necessity: for God loveth a cheerful giver. And God is able to make all grace abound toward you; that ye, always having all sufficiency in all things, may abound to every good work: (as it is written, He hath dispersed abroad; he hath given to the poor: his righteousness remaineth for ever. Now he that ministereth seed to the sower both minister bread for your food, and multiply your seed sown, and increase the fruits of your righteousness;) being enriched in every thing to all bountifulness, which causeth through us thanksgiving to God.

2 CORINTHIANS 9:6–11

❦

Although many folks are convinced that by pointing out their loved ones' flaws they are building them into their ideal of a perfect person, in reality, they often create Frankenstein instead. It's a self-fulfilling prophecy. We believe something so much (whether it's grounded in reality or not) and then act as if it were true, only to find it actually comes to pass.

Scripture teaches the repercussions of dwelling on the negative:

❦

Be not deceived; God is not mocked: for whatsoever a man soweth, that shall he also reap. For he that soweth to his flesh shall of the flesh reap corruption; but he that soweth to the Spirit shall of the Spirit reap life everlasting. And let us not be weary in well doing: for in due season we shall reap, if we faint not. As we have therefore opportunity, let us do good unto all men, especially unto them who are of the household of faith.

GALATIANS 6:7–10

Marianne made it a point whenever possible to mention that her young son was exactly like his father. And this, mind you, was not a compliment. "He's such a liar—just like his dad," she'd angrily ramble on. "I'm sure he'll end up in prison when he's grown."

Trust me; I'm not making this up. Can you imagine what those cruel words did to this young boy's self-esteem? After friends took her aside one afternoon and asked why she wanted to place such dire predictions about her young boy, she replied, "I'm trying to make him stand up and become a better individual by forcing him to prove that I'm wrong."

Interestingly enough, her older son (whom she had often praised) grew up an honor student and eventually become a successful practicing attorney. The younger boy, while not a convict as his mother had direly predicted, has continued to struggle with his personal as well as career goals. He's more or less a lost young man. Tell me, are you at all surprised? To this day, instead of believing she contributed to the problem, Marianne sees the outcome as proof that she was right about her son all along.

Do you know anyone who feels that if she criticizes her spouse, she'll improve his character or behavior? I can assure you that shaming someone into change, whether it be major weight loss, remembering your birthday, or calling home when he's going to be late, is not the best method of operation. Are these concerns necessary to address? Are they legitimate issues? Of course. However, it's always best to approach your spouse with love rather than judgment. Being positive, believing and hoping for the best, will bring you much faster and stronger results than will humiliating each other into alternative ways of thinking. Never allow extreme, vicious criticism—"You can't ever do anything right"—to bring you further away from your goal for an improved relationship than you were before.

Here's an important thought to consider: Self-fulfilling prophecies can be positive, too. Look at our previous scenario: Remember the mom who had criticized her youngest son? Remember she had also built up the oldest with praise and faith. Of course, she'll tell you she did this because she was just rewarding his already positive behavior. I'm sure some of that is true. Yet because she had offered him all her confidence that he would do well in life, he soaked it up, believed her, and sure enough, set out to make her prophecy come true.

Here's another example of the power of positive thinking. Over the last decade, Lynn gained about 40 pounds. No, this didn't happen by magic, nor did she inherit "fat genes." It occurred the typical way—by simply making poor food choices for extended periods of time. She doesn't blame her weight gain on pregnancies because fortunately she understands the truth.

Oddly enough, when Lynn first began to gain weight, she still saw herself as a thin person, one who had temporarily lapsed into a different body frame. However, over time, she became so accustomed to being overweight that she began to see herself as a different woman entirely. In Lynn's mind, she was no longer a slender individual who had unfortunately gained weight; she was now a heavy woman—end of story. Since Lynn now viewed herself in a negative light, she found that rather than being motivated to eat properly and lose the excess weight, the opposite proved to be true. Instead, Lynn thought about food, talked about food, and you guessed it, ate too much food as often as possible.

One day, when she finally realized that she was sowing an unhealthy attitude and therefore reaping an unhealthy body, Lynn began to put Scripture into action. Adhering to a friend's advice, she decided to think more like a thin person. It may sound strange, but she swears it actually worked. Lynn tried a little experiment. When she approached food, she believed that she was already thin. She imagined herself healthy, and what do you know, she began to react as a slender person would. For example, when Lynn saw a giant piece of chocolate pie, instead of shouting "hallelujah," gobbling it all up, and then looking for more, she made a little face (you know, the one that slender people often make when they see too much on their plates). She'd sigh heavily, as if the thought of eating pie was a tremendous chore, and say to herself, "Oh my, that looks soooo rich. I don't think I could possibly eat more than a couple bites." Then, guess what happened? Lynn found herself taking a taste or two and then pushing the ooey-gooey dessert aside, just as slender people do. And you know what? It actually worked. She really didn't want the rest of the pie. She didn't have to force it from her sight at all. In reality, a changed attitude, one that believed the best, made that delicious pie simply too much for one person to eat in one sitting. The result? Lynn lost weight, and she insists it was pretty darn easy.

The lesson? Believing in the positive—dwelling on it and then acting on it—will always bring more blessed results into your life than if you search for problems and dwell on the negative.

So, although it's important to address concerns in your marriage, be sure to mention all the things your spouse does right along with the areas you feel need improvement. Is he conscientious, loyal, kind, responsible, loving? Then be sure to mention your appreciation frequently.

❧

Love is a canvas furnished by Nature and embroidered by imagination.

VOLTAIRE

❧

By bringing his positive traits to the forefront, you will find that those qualities will grow like a tenderly nurtured garden while the negative behaviors fade into the background. Create a self-fulfilling prophecy that blesses your marriage, not one that creates your worst nightmare.

BELIEVE AND HOPE FOR YOUR FUTURE

Set aside time to examine your personal goals as well as your long-term hopes for your marriage. Then ask your mate to do the same. Now, compare notes. And for goodness sake, unless you're engaged to your clone, don't expect the lists to be exactly the same. However, if your idea of a perfect life is living in the country, raising ten children, and growing everything you eat while your partner desires to live in the big city and work his way up the corporate ladder, and his closest notion of having children is to pat the nieces and nephews on their heads once a year at the annual family Christmas gathering, you have some serious talking to do. You may be able to work some things out, make compromises, and set goals that please both of you. But you may find you're simply too far apart to make a match.

If you're like typical couples, though, you'll find that many of your goals are fairly similar, at least in spirit if not in every last detail. Once you've decided what your mutual goals are, you're on your way to achieving them. Follow up by supporting those dreams—by hoping and believing in both your desires. Yes, many dreams take years to completely come to pass, but with hope and faith and good old-fashioned determination, most will occur within your lifetime.

Instead of dwelling on the negative—"We'll never get out of this apartment and fulfill our desires of owning a home"—paint a picture of your dream in your mind, hope for it, pray for it, work hard toward it, and then wait patiently for it to come true. Always believe in God's goodness, believe in your dreams, and believe in each other.

GET RID OF THE BAGGAGE

Building a healthy relationship takes time, especially when old wounds come back to haunt you. Many times, these hurtful feelings are not caused by your spouse at all; they're simply old baggage from past relationships. They can be emotions stemming from prior romances or from negative family ties that are still too painful to forget.

I have several friends who are actively looking for someone to fall in love with. They insist they want a deep relationship. They swear they crave it. In fact, they assure everyone around them that they are on a long and determined search for love. In many cases, they even make clear their desire to get married. Yet each time one of them goes on a date, she finds a slew of reasons why the guy is absolutely WRONG for them. Over the years, I've heard them all: "He is too tall. He is too short. He isn't smart. He thinks he's too smart. He's too shy. He's too arrogant." In fact, sometimes it gets as petty as, "You wouldn't believe the shoes he wore. I just couldn't possibly get serious about anyone who has such horrible taste in footwear."

As silly as some of these issues sound, you might be surprised by how often they are nothing more than fear-based excuses generated by those looking for reasons NOT to fall in love. Oh, they may say they want intimacy, but in reality, they might fear it immensely. Why? Perhaps it's that old baggage again. They may shy away because of the potential of being hurt or the fear of commitment.

Trust me; I understand. When I was dating my husband, I decided he was simply too easygoing to marry. Yes, you heard me right. Too easygoing. And believe it or not, I thought my rationale made perfect sense. In fact, one evening after I'd returned from a lovely dinner with Patrick, I called one of my single friends and went on and on for thirty minutes about why this relationship was never going to work in a million years. "He never argues," I complained. "He's so calm; it's just boring!" My friend, also single and also looking for excuses not to commit while claiming she was desperately looking for love, began to fuel my fire. "Oh, I know exactly what you mean," she said. "I couldn't handle it either. That sort of boring calmness would absolutely drive me nuts!"

Finally, in the midst of my long-winded rambling, she came to her senses, stopped cold, and began to speak words of wisdom that changed the entire course of my life. "Oh my goodness, Candy," she went on to say, "just listen to yourself. What you are actually saying is you can't marry him because he's too nice!"

Of course that wasn't it, I insisted, she'd simply missed the depth of my valid complaints. But when I tried to explain myself and justify my attitude, I discovered in sudden powerful waves of reality that my friend was absolutely right! What in the world is wrong with me, I thought, that I need to find a reason to run from such a wonderful man? That conversation opened my eyes to something I'd been doing for years, and thankfully it changed my life forever. From that moment on, I began to ask myself, and pray about, what I was truly afraid of and why I had this inner need to pick apart everyone who might be the one for me while claiming I was looking for love. If it were not for my friend's words of inspired wisdom, I don't know if I would ever have caught on to my own destructive behavior, nor do I know if I would have had the blessing of seventeen glorious years of marriage to this "too nice" man.

DON'T BE SUPERFICIAL

Another way folks shun hope and belief and choose to run from relationships is by being superficial in their judgments. During Lori's college years, her friend dated a terrific young man. They were happy. They were in love, and they had joyously made plans to marry. However, when she brought him to meet Lori and their other gal pals, the women privately snickered behind their friend's back about what in the world she could possibly see in this man. After all, he had dared to commit a horrible fashion crime by wearing high-water plaid pants. (Hey, it was the '70s, but still, there was no excuse.) All the other women (still single, by the way) felt their friend had "settled" far too quickly for someone they knew couldn't possibly be good enough. What exactly was her problem, they pondered? Was she truly that desperate?

Fortunately for this gal, she ignored the opinions of her negative but well-meaning friends and went on to do the smart thing. She convinced her guy to buy new pants. Gee, how simple was that? The result? A great-looking, wonderful man, who has been her loving husband for a couple decades. In fact, to this day, every time Lori sees them together, she smiles at her initial judgment. If it had been up to her, the pants alone would have ended her friend's relationship right then and there.

The moral of this story? Wardrobes are easy to change, but character is not. Get past the superficial and analyze what your real motive for negativity is. Then, if you're honestly serious about dating, engagement, and marriage, concentrate on what really counts. After all, at the end of the day you'll know, just as Lori's friend did, when the love of your life has finally arrived. Plaid pants or not, grab him and run!

Always remember to prayerfully work on letting old fears go; then seek out acceptance and move toward your new life and purpose together.

BUILD TRUST

Never give your partner a reason to doubt your commitment. How many people have you met who love to taunt their mates by flirting with others? "It's harmless fun," they insist, but clearly, the repercussions are anything but helpful to their relationships. Perhaps they do it to get a rise out of their spouses, to make their spouses appreciate them more, or to keep from being taken for granted. To that I say, "Good luck!" No matter what the excuse, it's never a smart idea to cause someone you love to doubt your sincerity toward them. Instead, build trust, hope, and belief, and help your spouse to know there's deep inner faith supporting your commitment.

Building trust and faith requires making certain your spouse knows you're in the marriage for a lifetime. Of course we all have deal breakers—unfaithfulness and abuse can destroy a relationship in a heartbeat—but make sure your partner knows you can be trusted to stick with him through lesser, yet possibly frustrating, matters, such as financial trouble, illness, periods of boredom, or when the romance seems to have gone flat.

Have you ever gone to a wedding where the bride and groom stated, "Til we no longer love do we part"? Yikes, I have. I'm telling you, when I first heard the strange, somewhat wimpy vows, I was pretty convinced these folks weren't going to make it much past the reception. (The "union" did survive a few years longer than my estimate, but I'm sure you get the point.)

Remember, love is filled with emotion, and certain feelings may come and go during a lifetime of commitment. However, letting your spouse know you are there even when times get rough leads to a stronger relationship based on sincere hope and trust.

BE INTROSPECTIVE

Are you naturally a positive, faith-filled individual? Or are you like me—someone who tends to be rather fearful and negative? If you happen to fall into the latter category, relax: You can learn to change.

I vividly remember taking the initial premarital counseling required by our church. In it, Patrick and I were asked to take a basic personality test. Immediately, I began to wonder what this minister was up to. Sensing my fears, he calmly explained that he'd never scored a test and told anyone they shouldn't marry; he simply used it as a tool to reveal where troubles may naturally arise. Okay, fine, since I was sure at this point I wasn't going to be thrown out of the "engagement club," I agreed to cooperate.

The questionnaire asked for our perspectives and reactions to several everyday life scenarios, such as "When someone compliments you, do you internally question their sincerity?" The questions were not specific to our relationship but were simply intended to reveal our take on life in general. The answer options were "yes," "no," or "I'm not certain."

The following week, after the tests had been scored, the minister met with my fiancé and me. Smiling, he quietly informed us that, unfortunately, I needed to take the test again. Surely, he must be mistaken, I thought. He couldn't be talking about my test. But, yes, much to my embarrassment, he was. Shortly afterward, he went on to explain that in all the years he'd administered this exam, he'd never once had results come back marked "unscorable." The problem in a nutshell? I had answered too many questions with "I'm not certain." Apparently, I was too evasive for their automatic scoring system to grasp my personality type at all. Actually, that in itself should have told them a lot. I've always had great difficulty making decisions. I often see so many sides to an issue that I go on to analyze every detail to death and therefore can't come to a fair and logical conclusion.

Knowing he was right, I sheepishly agreed to retake it. To this day, my loving husband refers to this as the time I "flunked" my personality test.

When I took the exam for the second time, I forced myself to make clear choices (which, by the way, wasn't easy; there are so many ways to view these types of questions). Then, the scores were tallied. The results? Patrick is an easygoing, positive person, and I'm a big old, negative worrywart.

The minister smiled and explained none of this was a problem. (Did I really see Patrick lean forward as if considering a quick lunge for the door?) It was simply something we'd have to watch out for in the years to come. Down the line, he explained, Patrick would offer the positive side to life, bringing his dreams and visions for our relationship, and I would quickly pop his balloons as fast as he could blow them up. Did the minister's test turn out to be true? Actually, I'm ashamed to admit that it did—almost to the letter.

However, through prayer and the eyes of faith, and occasionally with my husband's gentle reminders, I've worked hard at seeing the positive in life even when my first instinct is to assume the worst.

In fact, this came up after the birth of my first child, Tiffany. She was experiencing minor knee pain off and on for a week. So I brought her in for a physical checkup. Almost immediately, I took the doctor aside and whispered, "Can you do a scan to make sure she doesn't have bone cancer?" In a flash, he did a double take, apparently trying to figure out how I could jump from teeny-weeny bouts of knee pain to life-threatening disease, and said, "I can assure you, in most cases these things are nothing more than plain old growing pains. Always look for the simple answer, not the horrible, complicated one." Then he added something I'll never forget: "When you hear the sounds of hooves trotting behind you, look for horses, not zebras." Yes, he was right. It's not usually the bizarre, terrible things that come our way; it's typically the mundane, simple situations that, in most cases, we can believe will turn out for the best.

Over the years, I've worked on trusting that good will come our way, knowing full well that on occasion, life throws us all some fairly ugly curveballs. Through prayer and by being aware that my nature is rather pessimistic to begin with, I'm able to maintain hope and faith. I understand now that having faith and seeing the positive in life are keys to a happy and well-adjusted marriage.

None without hope e'er lov'd the brightest fair,
But love can hope where reason would despair.

LORD LYTTLETON

BELIEVE AND HOPE IN GOD

We all need a foundation for our relationships, for our very purpose in being. Place your hope and faith in God as your personal beacon; then allow him to guide you through the rough spots of your marriage.

Hope, like the gleaming taper's light,
Adorns and cheers our way;
And still, as darker grows the night,
Emits a brighter ray.

OLIVER GOLDSMITH

By centering your marriage with faith in each other but more importantly with faith in God, you allow the Creator to uplift your union, bless your marriage, and guide you to places where you couldn't go on your own.

Scripture teaches that prayer can make an enormous difference. Nothing is too hard for God.

❧

And Jesus answering saith unto them, Have faith in God. For verily I say unto you, That whosoever shall say unto this mountain, Be thou removed, and be thou cast into the sea; and shall not doubt in his heart, but shall believe that those things which he saith shall come to pass; he shall have whatsoever he saith. Therefore I say unto you, What things soever ye desire, when ye pray, believe that ye receive them, and ye shall have them.

MARK 11:22−24

❧

To nurture this aspect of your soul, set time away from your busy schedule to pray and ask for faith inspiration. Then, if your spouse is willing, also make time to pray together to bring a closeness to your marriage that might otherwise be missed.

❧ *Accentuate the positive.* Think of things you can tell your spouse that are uplifting, that support their positive characteristics. Remind him of your appreciation for all he actually does right. Of course, address all concerns that need improvement, but never forget to compliment what you do like about him. If you have trouble thinking of enough good things, grab a piece of paper and begin to write down all the things your partner does (no matter how small) that you are grateful for. Dwell on these attributes, and most importantly, share them with each other.

❧ *Believe and hope for your future.* Set aside time for goal making, individually and as a couple. Then, work toward those goals, believe in their fruition, pray for God's help to bring them to pass, and chart your progress along the way, no matter how small.

❧ *Get rid of the baggage.* Look at your past in detail. Analyze your family life, your security issues, and your prior relationships. Then, unpack those bags. Begin to see your present attitude as one that may have been influenced by past disappointments, loss, and letdowns. Prayerfully approach your marriage with newness and fresh eyes. After all, isn't that how we want to be treated? Never make your spouse the victim of old anger that should have been dispersed elsewhere along the way.

¶ *Don't be superficial.* If you find yourself judging your mate through the eyes of pettiness, prayerfully discover what your true reasons for doing so might be. Could it actually be fear of intimacy and fear of commitment that cause you to push others away over things that don't really matter in the larger scheme of life? Begin to approach your relationship with an attitude of refusing to make molehills into mountains. Always let the trivial remain just that while concentrating on important issues such as commitment, trust, and love.

¶ *Build trust.* Pray to overcome old baggage that keeps you from fully trusting someone new. Never give your spouse reason to doubt your loyalty and commitment. Don't play with fire by flirting or threatening to leave simply for the sake of drama. Only commit to someone you know can be trusted. Never fall for the belief you can change anyone's basic internal character.

- *Be introspective.* Know your personality type. In most cases, you don't have to take a test to come to a basic understanding of whether you're positive or negative by nature. Most of your friends can tell you your personality type in a heartbeat if you only dare to ask. If you're positive, make sure your husband sees that by lifting him up every chance you can. If you tend to be negative, understand that that may color your perspective, and weigh that factor before you make assumptions that may not be based in fairness.

- *Believe and hope in God.* Make time for quiet prayer and meditation. Ask God for guidance and a new perspective to fill you with hope and belief in your marriage. If your spouse is willing, spend time together in prayer, which can result in a deeper level of unity that only God can provide.

VII.

Love Never Fails

Enduring Love—most of us long for it, seek it, pray for it, and hope deep in our hearts that such a gift truly exists.

At the touch of love, everyone becomes a poet.

PLATO

So many people have been disappointed when the feelings of love from the early stages of their relationships faded, leaving them with nothing more than shattered memories. Is it any wonder that they continuously ask themselves, Does enduring love truly exist? Of course it does. And this may come as a surprise to some, but love doesn't happen by magic when Cupid fires his random shot; nor does it occur just to the lucky. In actuality, love exists solely among those willing to make a conscious decision to see this virtue fulfilled.

BE LED BY YOUR COMMITMENT

Isn't it interesting that many folks who are sure they've met "the one," go on to fall in love with those cute little characteristics they just adore ("The way he looks down in shyness when he talks…") but soon those very characteristics drive them absolutely crazy! Before long, we're doomed to hear cries of, "Why doesn't he look me in the eye when we're having a conversation?" Our desire to maintain our vows of commitment must mean not looking for excuses as to why the individuals we swore just a couple years ago to love forever now annoy us too much to bother keeping around.

For those who feel they've been given a sign that they've found their soul mates, they may have stronger evidence to believe their relationships are truly right. When I was young and single, I prayed for God to send a wonderful man, and I was fairly specific. I wanted him to be tall, dark, and handsome, with an exotic accent. Looking back, I realize I should have left the list wide open for God to fill, but in my case, guess what? He blessed every dream I had. Now, I could assume God answered my prayer, or perhaps knowing full well that he wanted this match to occur in the first place, God placed that desire in my heart and not the other way around. Yes, sometimes we think we're the head when we're actually the tail.

Since I prayerfully asked God to lead my decisions and asked sincerely for him to stop me anywhere along the way if I started down the wrong path, I firmly believed his desire was that my husband and I should marry.

Now, years later, this gives me a great deal of confidence to make my marriage work. When I add that to the vow I took before my husband, others, and yes, even to God himself, I know I'm heading down the right track toward lifelong commitment.

I recently spoke with a wonderful woman who met her husband in an unusual way—over the Internet. Before people cringe in horror, remember that in many ways, this is just the modern-day way to be pen pals. And for the record, she's been happily married to this fellow for several years now.

One day, after they finally met in person and were on a casual date, she prayed for God's guidance. She'd known men before who seemed nice, only to discover later that the relationships were dismal mistakes. She told me that immediately after her prayer, she heard a quiet voice state, "He's a good man. Don't be afraid." Now in case you're wondering, no, my friend's not crazy. She simply asked for reassurance, and God graciously offered it in a sacred and special way. Once she knew her instincts were not misleading her, the two continued to date and soon were engaged and married. My friend knows now, without a shadow of a doubt, that her choice to commit was divinely orchestrated, so she's never allowed petty differences or doubts to get in the way of the blessings of their future.

So, rather than allowing the emotions of the moment to lead your marriage, make a conscious decision to have your vows guide you instead. Most folks understand that feelings may come and go. There are days you may feel wildly in love, absolutely certain your relationship was the best choice you could have made. There will be days, however, when you'll look at each other and wonder how in the world you ever made a match in the first place. By allowing emotions and feelings of romance, or lack thereof, to guide your life, you may find it nearly impossible to fulfill your commitment.

Mark spent a lazy afternoon with his grandparents in their Arizona home. At the time, they were both in their 80s and had been married approximately sixty years. Feeling rather sarcastic, and a bit feisty, his grandmother leaned over the table, looked at her husband, and in a silly way said, "Who is that man? Why did I marry him? I'm not sure I know him at all." No, senility had not set in. Mark's grandma was simply asking that age-old question "What in the world have I gotten myself into?" Of course, Mark laughed and said, "It's way too late for philosophical questions like that now, Grandma. You should have wondered about that stuff years ago." And his grandfather? He just grinned, rolled his eyes, and continued nonchalantly eating lunch. Oh, the drama of it all.

So, if you're able to recognize the vital importance of your commitment to your marriage vows, your spouse, God, and the inner voice of your heart and you understand that minus any unacceptable personal deal breakers you are in this union for life, you will stand apart from a somewhat confused and fickle crowd.

Scripture teaches us to take our vows seriously:

Be not rash with thy mouth, and let not thine heart be hasty to utter any thing before God: for God is in heaven, and thou upon earth: therefore let thy words be few. For a dream cometh through the multitude of business; and a fool's voice is known by multitude of words. When thou vowest a vow unto God, defer not to pay it; for he hath no pleasure in fools: pay that which thou hast vowed. Better is it that thou shouldest not vow, than that thou shouldest vow and not pay. Suffer not thy mouth to cause thy flesh to sin; neither say thou before the angel, that it was an error: wherefore should God be angry at thy voice, and destroy the work of thine hands? For in the multitude of dreams and many words there are also divers vanities: but fear thou God.

ECCLESIASTES 5:2-7

Those whose marriages succeed typically grasp that their conscious decision is what keeps them happily together. They make a choice to be happy, a choice to stay together, and a choice to protect a vital, enduring relationship.

In contrast, those who allow their emotions to guide them typically find themselves enduring a roller-coaster relationship, one that often crashes unnecessarily.

Although your own decision is important, a commitment toward enduring love must be mutual. When it's not, one-half of the couple cannot force success upon the other. Many people (mostly women, I must say) feel that through prayer, personal growth, begging, pleading, you name it, they can convince their spouses to stay committed to their marriages. Although I admire their sheer and genuine determination to work things out, in many cases, they unfortunately fail miserably. Why, you may ask? Because we all have a gift, and it's called free will.

If you're married to an individual who views life differently and who is led by his emotions and not his vows, you can reach out and try to save the relationship, but the ultimate outcome is in his hands. Although honest attempts at reconciliation, prayer, and faith are worthy choices, in the end, you cannot control the freewill nature of your mate. He will make his own decision. Why? Because God made him that way. He gave each and every one of us free will, and all the attempts or prayers on your part may nfluence your husband's decision but will not take away his right to choose.

Many individuals become angry at God because their attempts at praying, begging, and pleading for their marriages did not reap the results they had hoped for. After a horrible divorce, they often blame God for refusing to fulfill their desires. Yet ultimately, that decision was never in God's hands at all. Yes, God's plan is clear, but he allows all of us the choice to follow his greater plan or to deviate from it. Unfortunately, the times when people need their faith and the deepest comfort of God the most, such as in the midst of a devastating broken relationship, are often when they turn away from faith out of bitterness. Instead of blaming God for your spouse's decisions, allow God's gentle spirit to be your comfort through the difficulties life may throw your way.

Believe it or not, there are no magic secrets. We're all given a fair shot at happiness. No one's born lucky in love. Granted, some of us may have had a rough start in life and may not have been offered a wonderful example of commitment. Perhaps you've come from a long line of divorce, and you've never experienced enduring love except by watching it in the movies. You might be surprised to learn that those who succeed in love are in a relationship in which both partners have made a commitment to see it succeed. When it fails, one or both of them have decided they were no longer interested in pursuing love together.

Maybe someone sabotaged the relationship. Maybe someone walked out. Maybe someone committed the one cardinal sin he knew his partner would consider a deal breaker. But without a doubt, somebody turned the tables on his vows. The destruction of relationships does not happen by accident. It may occur slowly and in a subtle fashion. Or it may happen suddenly; but clearly, someone makes a choice along the way.

How many people do you know who choose to have an affair, knowing full well they're placing their marriages on the line? Yet how often do we see them cry when those very marriages come screeching to an end? Interesting, isn't it? The choice they made shows they were willing to risk their relationships, that they were willing to pay the ultimate price. Perhaps it was an unconscious sabotage of commitments they wanted out of in the first place. Perhaps they foolishly thought they could get away with it, sort of have their cake and eat it too. Regardless, they made a conscious decision to walk away from their vows, risking the total destruction of their marriages.

LEAVE AN ENDURING LEGACY

Instead of leaving a trail of destruction and devastating our children or others watching, why not leave a legacy of enduring love for others to follow? Too much pressure, you say? Not really. I'm not implying a perfect, we've-never-had-an-argument-in-our-lives kind of relationship. I'm talking about a lasting commitment to love. Rather than offering our children and those who might know us an example of another reason "love doesn't last," show them through mutual faith, commitment, and determination that it most certainly can. Be that beam of light others can follow through the darkness.

Scripture teaches us of the importance of setting an example for the world:

❧

Ye are the salt of the earth: but if the salt have lost his savour, wherewith shall it be salted? It is thenceforth good for nothing, but to be cast out, and to be trodden under foot of men. Ye are the light of the world. A city that is set on an hill cannot be hid. Neither do men light a candle, and put it under a bushel, but on a candlestick; and it giveth light unto all that are in the house. Let your light so shine before men, that they may see your good works, and glorify your Father which is in heaven.

MATTHEW 5:13–16

❧

As others see marriages that do endure, it gives them strength to know it can happen. During college, Marta dated a man who was emotionally abusive. She had dreams of a relationship based on commitment, trust, and enduring love. Her boyfriend came close to convincing her that she was living in a fairy-tale world, until one day when Marta met a group of people at church who appeared to have loving, caring marriages based on trust, commitment, and respect. It was at this point that she realized her boyfriend was a liar. Of course, she's sure now none of those marriages were actually perfect.

However, Marta began to have faith for something far better than she had previously been settling for. Soon afterward, she left this man and went out in search of someone with similar values as her own. Approximately six years later, she met her husband. They were married a year later, and Marta knows now that her instincts were always right. Enduring love is possible—if you and your spouse choose for it to be.

If you grew up in a home influenced by divorce, personal scars may make it harder for you to believe that love can endure. Just always remember that you are neither your parents nor your friends; you are who God made you and who you choose to be. So while it may be harder for you to believe in enduring love, trust the fact that the only things that really count are your commitment, your spouse's commitment, and your faith in God to see you both through.

COMFORT THE BROKENHEARTED

When marriages fail around you (and without a doubt, they will), instead of inflicting unfair judgment, lovingly offer others the comfort that hope is truly available. Just because their marriages failed this time does not mean they won't discover and experience nurturing, enduring love in the future.

A few years ago, Karen came to her friends with news that she and her husband of many years were about to divorce. Her friends were shocked. In fact, they quietly questioned her reasoning for wanting to leave such a wonderful man. After all, everyone has problems, and didn't she make a vow to stay together always? Was it any of their business? No. But did they still feel compelled to judge her choice? You bet. And as it turned out, they were wrong. Much to Karen's good sense, she left her husband anyway.

Approximately a year later, she began to tell her friends the whole story—how her husband had verbally abused her constantly during their twenty-year marriage, calling her horrid names and accusing her of things she'd never even think of doing. As all the truth came pouring out, it was clear that this woman had tolerated far more than any of her friends could ever have dreamed of. Her ex-husband was a menace and a cruel individual.

In the end, no matter how much we think we know about another's situation, give her the benefit of the doubt, because she always knows more. Ultimately, whether her reasons are justified or not is solely between her and God. The truth is, no one, not even her closest friends, will ever know the whole story. Perhaps her spouse made a freewill choice to destroy their relationship. Perhaps she too will grow in understanding any part she may have played in the breakup. But none of this means her future is forever branded and set for failure. If she is willing to grow and make wise choices, always leaning on faith to guide her, her past does not need to dictate her future.

Scripture encourages us to offer healing words, prayers, and hope to others:

The Spirit of the Lord GOD is upon me;
Because the LORD hath anointed me to preach good tidings
*   unto the meek;*

He hath sent me to bind up the brokenhearted,
To proclaim liberty to the captives,
And the opening of the prison to them that are bound;
To proclaim the acceptable year of the LORD,
And the day of vengeance of our God;
To comfort all that mourn;
To appoint unto them that mourn in Zion,
To give unto them beauty for ashes,
The oil of joy for mourning,
The garment of praise for the spirit of heaviness;
That they might be called trees of righteousness,
The planting of the LORD, that he might be glorified.
And they shall build the old wastes,
They shall raise up the former desolations,
And they shall repair the waste cities,
The desolations of many generations....
For your shame ye shall have double;
And for confusion they shall rejoice in their portion:
Therefore in their land they shall possess the double:
Everlasting joy shall be unto them.

ISAIAH 61:1–7

MAKE LOVE LAST

Have you ever had a friend put you on hold because the annoying beeping of Call Waiting beckoned them away? And even worse, has she ever told you that she'd have to hang up because the other call took priority over yours? Well, I have heard that, and I can tell you, it's rather disheartening to realize that I'm not making the cut on her telephone priority list.

How many of you have had a friend cancel a get-together because someone else came along and offered her an exciting date instead? Sorry, but your casual movie plans are no match for the new guy she's been dying to go out with. Isn't that lovely when you're trumped by someone your friend decides is more important than you?

Likewise, for some folks, their commitment to their marriages is nothing more than a temporary arrangement until better partners come along. This may be fine for dating, but once you've uttered the marriage vows, you should never be seriously tempted by others trying to steal your love away. Be loyal to your commitment, or don't make it at all. Let your spouse know that he is number one and that that's not just a short-term condition until someone better comes strolling by.

Beyond making a commitment and expressing desire to keep your marriage everlasting, it's wise to offer joy and freshness to your relationship. We all fall into old, dull life routines: watching endless television, eating the same meals, falling into the trap of talking only about the kids or the infamous, annoying dripping faucet. It's always wise to bring new life back to your relationship.

Of course, the reality is that marriage is not dating; it's not a romance novel in which rose petals line your every step to the bedroom. And anyone who thinks it is is only asking for disappointment. Still, it's smart to bring yourselves away from routine whenever possible. A night out for dinner without the kids splashing spaghetti all over your clothes, a quiet, quick getaway to the coast, or a simple mug of refreshment at your local coffee shop while you chat together for an hour will bring joy and pep back into a tired relationship.

SHAKE THINGS UP

Are you stuck in a rut with your attitude, your look, and even your personality? Don't we all desire a total television-talk-show makeover? How about shaking up more than your hairdo or your wardrobe?

Trust me, every now and then even I get bored with myself. I've colored my hair from brunet to red to (most recently) blond. Okay, I admit that on a few occasions, it's accidentally turned out a scary shade of orange. There are days my husband comes home from work and he's not quite sure who he's going to meet. Will I have short hair or long; blond hair or red? Will I decide to change jobs or write another book? Will I be in a romantic mood or saying I have a headache? If nothing else, it keeps things interesting.

Why not shake things up now and then? Without a doubt, it will keep your relationship fresh and protect you from boring yourself along the way. What about taking a creative class, joining a club, meeting new friends, or spending more time with those you've known for years but often get too busy to see? Take yourself off the go-to-work, come-home, drop-the-kids-at-soccer bandwagon and create a new and interesting life based on your own growing desires. Clearly, by doing so, you'll become more confident, and more interesting, to yourself as well as your spouse.

DON'T TRY TOO HARD

In the attempt to bring joy back to your relationship, refrain from over-planning or creating a sense of overexpectation. Years ago, on my honeymoon, my husband and I made arrangements to stay in a lovely hotel in Carmel. Thinking I'd bring romance into full bloom, I brought wonderfully scented bubble bath for the Jacuzzi tub included in our room.

Unbeknownst to me, it's never wise to put zesty suds into the agitation of a Jacuzzi. (Am I the only person on earth who didn't know this?) Unfortunately, having been accustomed to the difficulty of keeping bubbles afloat in a typical bath, I decided to use the whole bottle. (Yes, I swear, the entire thing.)

I'm sure you've guessed what happened—we were immediately inundated by giant, concentrated bubbles that exploded ferociously from the vibrating machine, landing wherever they could, littering the room around us. Once we realized the suds had overflowed their luxurious marble container and had poured onto the floor, flowing toward the bed, we panicked. We tried everything. We added water. It only made them worse. We tried hitting them with towels, but that didn't work either. Let me assure you, those suds were unpoppable!

Eventually, feeling frustrated and a bit worried as to what the maid might think, we went to the kitchen (fully stocked within our suite) and pulled out a large spaghetti pot. We filled the stainless-steel container with bubbles and tried distributing them throughout the room. We placed them in the shower, in the kitchen sink, and even out onto the deck, where most of them remained, though a clever few managed to float in large, chunky lumps out to sea. For a moment, it looked like it was snowing in California!

And my husband? Was he still in the mood for romance? Not exactly. Feeling as if he was caught up in an I Love Lucy episode rather than a romantic flick, he laughed hysterically, grabbed my hand, and suggested we make a run for it. Not having any better ideas, I agreed. Together, we bolted from the hotel and spent several hours shopping in town. Late that evening, when we returned to our room, the suds were miraculously gone, a successful attempt, no doubt, by a determined maid who apparently owned an enormous bubble-popping machine.

Can I just say now that the entire episode was NOT what I had planned. Yet the happy memories of that weekend are still with us today. I share this with you, despite my husband's nervous objections, to express that things don't have to turn out picture-perfect to be beneficial to your relationship. Sometimes, just adding joy and fun to your life will instill more romance than well-crafted plans ever could.

Can't afford a weekend away? How about planning a simple date night? But even then, be careful. The first year or two of Renee and Rick's marriage, they made it a point to go out on the town every Friday night. This plan was initiated because Renee had read somewhere that it would keep their romance alive. It was actually a wonderful idea, but the first time Rick didn't feel like going out, the result was one big, whopping argument. Now how's that for romance? Through this experience, they both learned that in their effort to keep romance in full bloom, they had almost cut it off the vine.

Sometimes, you may miss a date night (ours are down to about one every few months now). Sometimes, he'll forget to bring flowers on your birthday, but ultimately, it's the larger picture—your commitment—that really matters. Never let perfectly constructed plans for romance be the reason to end that very romance when things don't go off exactly as you'd hoped. Instead, roll with the punches, let life throw you a few curves, and have a little fun. After all, whoever said life was perfect? Despite these imperfections, you can make your marriage blessed, fun, and most of all, enduring—if you want to. So work at it, but don't try too hard.

Remember these words:

❦

The vow that binds too strictly snaps itself.

ALFRED TENNYSON

❦

❦ TIPS TO TAKE AWAY ❦

§ *Be led by your commitment.* Make a conscious decision before the wedding and during the marriage that minus your personal deal breakers, you will pursue an enduring relationship. Ask your loved one to do the same. Commit your vows to your spouse, yourself, and your God. Be accountable to all three to see them through.

§ *Leave an enduring legacy.* Show the world, your friends, and your children that love can last. Be a light in an often dark and discouraging world. Never try to make your marriage appear perfect, but with humility, give people a reason to believe love can last for a lifetime. Offer your family, and even the world, hope rather than despair.

§ *Comfort the brokenhearted.* As you meet people around you suffering the loss of love or the destruction of their marriages, their hopes, and their dreams, never judge them; instead, offer comfort that through faith, they too will survive. Remind them they are not "unlucky," and their future doesn't need to be determined by their past.

¶ *Make love last.* Introduce fun back into your relationship. Don't allow boring routine to become a way of life. Set aside time to get away for the weekend or just for a quiet lunch. Make an attempt not to talk about the kids or the house, and open up your conversation beyond the usual. Bring home flowers, make your spouse's favorite dinner, offer up little surprises that will give you both joy.

¶ *Shake things up.* Every now and then, dare to bring a fresh approach to your life and therefore interject new feelings into your marriage. Take a class, change that tired look you've stuck with for the last twenty years, read a new book, and continue to grow and change until you've pulled yourself out of your own rut—and in return have breathed new life back into your relationship.

¶ *Don't try too hard.* In an attempt to break the monotony, don't place pressure on yourself or your spouse to provide the perfect moment, perfect getaway, or perfect evening. Understand that life often throws us strange and unexpected curves. So if at the last minute the car won't start, the sitter gets sick, or the Jacuzzi overflows, just roll with the punches. After all, in the end, sharing your love and nurturing your God-given blessings are really all that matters.

ACKNOWLEDGMENTS

I'd like to offer a special thanks to my wonderful editor, Paula Munier, for conceptualizing this project. Once again, you've been a joy to work with, Paula. Thank you so much for your support, encouragement, and enduring faith in my work.

ABOUT THE AUTHOR

ↄ

Candy Chand is the author of *Under God's Wings* and *Gift of Grace*. She coauthored *Ashley's Garden*—the inspirational account of one family's spiritual healing after the Oklahoma City bombing—and also penned the widely read story "Christmas Love." Chand lives in Northern California.